THE
PARK

LEARNING FROM DELHI

LEARNING FROM
DELHI
PRACTISING ARCHITECTURE IN URBAN INDIA

PELLE POIESZ • GERT JAN SCHOLTE
SANNE VANDERKAAIJ GANDHI

MAPIN PUBLISHING

First published in India in 2016 by
Mapin Publishing Pvt. Ltd
706 Kaivanna, Panchvati, Ellisbridge,
Ahmedabad 380006
T: 91 79 4022 8228 • F: 91 79 4022 8201
E: mapin@mapinpub.com
www.mapinpub.com

Photographs and illustrations © as listed below:
Bas Losekoot: Cover, endpapers, pp. 5, 11, 12, 14, 47–52, 76, 78, 92, 98–106, 112, 124, 138, 142–156, 192, 206, 218, 221
Pelle Poiesz and Gert Jan Scholte: pp. 134, 197
Shailen Parker: pp. 60, 61
André J. Fanthome: pp. 62, 64, 162, 178
Asim-Waqif: p. 174
Ilse van der Klei: pp. 31–37
All other photographs and illustrations were obtained from the interviewed architects and urbanists.

978-93-85360-12-1 (Mapin)
978-1-935677-69-7 (Grantha)
LCCN: 2016930632

Concept: Pelle Poiesz and Gert Jan Scholte (mail@learningfromindia.nl)
Text of Interviews: Sanne Vanderkaaij Gandhi
Design: studio ilse van klei (ilsevanklei.nl)
Production: Mapin Design Studio
Printed by Parksons Graphics, Mumbai

Learning from Delhi received funding from the **creative industries fund NL**

Front and back: View of Delhi from Jama Masjid mosque.

NEW DELHI MUNICIPAL COUNCIL (NDMC) BUILDING, PALIKA KENDRA, DELHI

CONTENTS

ARTICLES

INTERVIEWS

PREFACE

PELLE POIESZ
GERT JAN SCHOLTE
SANNE VANDERKAAIJ GANDHI

Pelle Poiesz (1971) was born in Dar es Salaam, Tanzania. He studied at Delft University of Technology (TU Delft) in the Netherlands and at the Sir J.J. College of Architecture in Mumbai. In 2000, together with Manou Huijbregts, he established the architectural firm HP architecten in Rotterdam (www.hparchitecten.nl). HP architecten is an all-round architectural office with a portfolio that ranges from housing, office, cultural and educational buildings, to fully detailed interior design. The office operates on the central premise that good design creates spaces in which the user feels welcome and at home, respected and inspired.

Gert Jan Scholte (1970) is an architect who studied at the Faculty of Architecture at TU Delft in the Netherlands and at the Sir J.J. College of Architecture in Mumbai. He is the co-founder of Cityblob, an Amsterdam-based architecture, urban planning and real estate development company with a particular focus on railway and underground stations and their surrounding areas. A recently realized project is CU! Amsterdam, a large-scale sport, retail and leisure development that is part of the new Amsterdam Bijlmer Arena railway station.

Sanne Vanderkaaij Gandhi (1979) completed an MA in (Non-Western) History at the University of Groningen and an MSc in Asian Studies at the University of Amsterdam (both in the Netherlands). She is finalizing her PhD thesis in International Development Studies at the University of Amsterdam, and works as a freelance researcher and writer. Sanne is based in Mumbai.

In 2013, when our journey of *Learning from Mumbai* concluded, we shifted our gaze towards India's capital. We soon started with the preparations for *Learning from Delhi*, the second volume in the series Learning from India. The same questions that led us to create *Learning from Mumbai* accompanied us while finding our way through this new city: What can we learn from the planning and architecture of Delhi? What can we learn from Delhi's architects and planners? What can we learn about–and moreover from–practising planning and architecture in Delhi?

Both Mumbai and Delhi are urban sprawls for which the word 'large' is far too modest. Both are mega-cities with populations of some 20 million inhabitants. Both are melting pots where people from all corners of India meet. Yet the differences between Mumbai and Delhi are bigger than their similarities. The cities differ immensely with regard to a great many observable matters, of which climate, geography, layout, planning and architecture styles, and rules and regulations are just a few. They also differ in a great number of ways which are more difficult to put into words, such as the mentality of their inhabitants, the governance styles of their bureaucrats, and the influence of their shorter (Mumbai) and longer (Delhi) histories on the present day.

During our subsequent visits to Delhi we stayed in various parts of the city. We travelled many kilometres by car, rickshaw, metro, and foot to meet a great variety of people working and living in the city, and to see and experience as many neighbourhoods as we could. Ultimately, we really got to know the metropolis thanks to the stories and observations shared with us by architects, planners, and others directly working in and on the city. With each story shared and each perspective elaborated upon, Delhi not only became more familiar, but also a place we slowly but surely began to fall in love with.

OUTLINE

This volume consists of three parts: a section with background articles, a section with interviews, and a photo essay.

We open with four background articles that provide an introduction to the city. The first article, by Dunu Roy gives an introduction to the historical and contemporary context for architecture and city planning in Delhi. Who makes cities? And who breaks them? These questions are relevant as all cities go through a phase of 'renewal'.

Ashok Bhalotra, in Moulding the Region to a New City, discusses urban planning and development in the context of the Delhi-Mumbai Industrial Corridor (DMIC). He explains his personal journey to draw up a master plan for New Neemrana; a plan that had to incorporate a staggering number of over forty existing villages.

If there is one modern architect who left a major impression on Delhi with his architecture, it would be Joseph Allen Stein (1912–2001). Exclusively for *Learning from Delhi*, Shyam Khandekar wrote an ode to this iconic architect:

'A Tribute to Joseph Allen Stein.' The architect reflects on his personal meetings with Stein, his work, and his legacy.

This section of the book concludes with an overview of some facts and figures on the city compiled by arch-i as well as various maps. These graphic representations of the city provide a beautiful illustration of the staggering growth that Delhi has witnessed.

In the next section we present some of the interviews we held with practising professionals in Delhi. During our three visits we met a wide variety of architects and planners. Some were engaged in projects on a mammoth scale, such as Mohit Gujral of DLF and Onno Ruhl and Barjor Mehta of the World Bank. Some were practitioners with decades of experience: Romi Khosla and the world famous Raj Rewal. Others presided over flourishing practices covering a plethora of project types: Ambrish Arora, Pankaj Gupta, Christine Mueller, Madhav Raman, and Sonali Rastogi. Pradip Krishen and Mohammad Shaheer made us shift our gaze from the usual steel, cement, and stone to the trees and plants of Delhi. Joerie Aulman and Anne Feenstra not only shared their professional knowledge of planning and architecture in and around Delhi, but–being Dutch–also provided us with their intercultural take on working in Delhi.

In this section you will also find a brief article on the workshop we conducted at the School of Planning and Architecture (SPA) in Delhi. Students reflected on the expected, the unexpected, the conspicuous, and the inconspicuous spatial impact of the highly successful Metro.

We asked Bas Losekoot to travel with us to Delhi and to shine his light and focus his lens on India's capital and its inhabitants. Who are the Delhiites? Who walks those wide pavements and visits the numerous green spaces? Who crowds the Metro and Delhi's tiny lanes? His photo essay does more than justice to this fascinating metropolis: his images celebrate the many faces of Delhi.

We hope that in the current volume you will not only find the answers to the questions that we were asking ourselves, but that you will also feel some of the spark we felt while interacting with so many of Delhi's interesting residents. We hope that you will be left feeling–just like we were–that you have learned from Delhi and want to keep Learning from Delhi.

Pelle Poiesz
Gert Jan Scholte
Sanne Vanderkaaij Gandhi

NATIONAL COOPERATIVE DEVELOPMENT CORPORATION (NCDC), DELHI

SHRI RAM CENTRE, DELHI

Shankar Lal Murli Dhar Auditorium
RAMKALI
Operation Three Star

INTER-STATE BUS TERMINUS, KASHMERE GATE, DELHI

SEMI DELUXE
nal Road Transport Corporation Kullu
SEMI DELUXE
HP 34A 7998

ARTICLES

ARTICLES
ARTICLES
ARTICLES
ARTICLES
ARTICLES
ARTICLES
ARTICLES
ARTICLES
ARTICLES
ARTICLES

CITY MAKERS AND CITY BREAKERS

DUNU ROY

Dunu Roy, formerly A.K. Roy, is a chemical engineer by training, social scientist by compulsion, and political ecologist by choice. He worked for over four decades on land and water management, secure settlements, safe work, environmental planning, leadership training, and pollution control in both rural and urban communities. His work is poised on the delicate borderline between environment and development. He is the founder of the Hazards Centre, which provides research support to community and labour organisations in Delhi.

Who makes cities? And who breaks them? These questions are relevant as all cities go through a phase of 'renewal'. The immediate response of most people would be that it is enlightened governments and rulers who make truly good cities, and that it is invaders, terrorists, and impoverished migrants who break them. But an instinctive reaction is not necessarily an indicator of reality, it could be a result of a mixture of propaganda and history; perhaps the 'truth' could even lie elsewhere. For cities have their own organic logic of growth. Different interests compete to make the city the way they want it. Those who fail to discover this central truth eventually end up seeing only their own needs as central to the city, at the cost of those whose lives are hidden beneath the grime and dirt on which the city is built. Nothing illustrates this better than the modern history of the city of Delhi

The visible structure of the city is imposed upon its social foundations. When even a casual visitor looks up at the imposing walls of the forts built by the Tughlaqs and the Mughals, it could occur to him that these walls could not have been actually 'built' by the kings. There must have been masons and stonecutters, water carriers and sand loaders, mixers and helpers, woodcutters and carpenters, ironsmiths and potters, labouring men and women and donkeys by the thousands who did the actual work. So where, in the pages of history, did they all disappear?

COMPANY POWER

The armed force on which the English built their power necessitated the planning and construction of barracks and Company quarters near every large town. The confluence of the ancient Grand Trunk Road and the newly commissioned Bombay-Agra Road in the first half of the nineteenth century made Delhi a place of crucial military importance. The aftermath of the Mutiny of 1857 led to further enforcement of control and the area around the Red Fort was cleared of the civilian population to enable the military to assert its supremacy. But what was this civilian population near the fort and why did it pose a threat to the new rulers? And why was the civil administration moved in 1912 to a Secretariat that was built far away from the fort, next to the Northern Ridge (near Metcalfe House, built in 1835 to house the Governor General's agent at the Mughal Court), within the safer confines of the Civil Lines? Did it have anything to do with distancing the bonded labouring classes from the reigning centre?

Immediately after the Mutiny it was also suggested by the British military commanders led by James Outram that the entire Walled City of Shahjahanabad be razed to the ground, but fortunately there was not enough explosive available for this task. While the Civil Lines for British administrators who took over power in 1803 had been laid out to the north of the Walled City, the Viceregal Lodge (now Delhi University) with its protective barracks was built in 1920 at an even safer distance from the subjugated 'natives', across and to the north-west of the Ridge. The imperatives of colonial rule were also reflected in the formation of the Delhi Municipal Committee in 1874. In the next decade the Committee proposed the construction of a commercial square outside the Walled City to the north, clearing the space for a new commercial quarter between Lahori Gate and Sadar Bazar, to be developed as a profitable enterprise in the tradition of the East India Company. The close of the century also saw the intrusion of the railway line as it broke through the ramparts of the Red Fort and Shahjahanabad. This new mode of transport began displacing the old trade routes with their sarais, since it generally followed the same alignments. So who was breaking and who was making the city?

EMPIRE AND EXCLUSION

The railways continued their expansion in the beginning of the twentieth century and, in the process, the new planners pulled down the bastions of the Walled City and filled the city's protective ditches and canals. Thus, Delhi Sadar station was constructed between the old town and Sadar Bazar, disrupting the organic linkage between the two, while a Mercantile Boulevard was proposed between the Kabuli and Ajmeri Gates—now celebrated as the decadent red light district of the city! It did not take long for the rulers to notice that a second, but lower class, city was organically growing in Paharganj (hillside market), Sadar Bazar (central market), and Sabzi Mandi (vegetable market) across the railway tracks. This led to the appointment of an Assistant Commissioner in 1908 as Officer on Special Duty to 'plan the future expansion of Delhi on an orderly basis'. This officer promptly recommended the westward expansion of the city across the Ridge and the 'improvement' of the older areas. By 1912, the dream of an Imperial city at Delhi was transformed into reality and a Town Planning Committee was appointed for the purpose.

This Committee oversaw the acquisition of extensive areas in the southern basin for the construction of an Imperial New Delhi. The architects Baker and Lutyens thus located the new Viceregal Palace (now Rashtrapati Bhavan) on the imposing height of Raisina hill with the new city spread out at its feet, to physically emphasise the difference between the rulers and the subjugated. Huge acreages were laid aside for the bureaucracy and ruling elite with spacious avenues and parks dominating the landscape. In the process much of the earlier drainage system, which had taken the run-off from the Aravalis to the tombs and gardens of the earlier rulers, was destroyed to make way for a new regime of storm-water drains. The Committee also decided to completely demolish the remaining city wall 'to provide access of air to the congested area'. This displaced a large number of artisans and workmen who lived near the city wall. So the Committee assigned the Western Extension Area (WEA) for expansion, particularly for settling the 'poorer classes'—or those who served the city with their labour. The railway line to the old capital of Kolkata also provided the pretext for forcibly acquiring prime agricultural land in 1915 from farmers on the east bank of the Yamuna river.

We get a glimpse of how an exclusive city was beginning to emerge when for the first time, in 1924, the Harphool Singh slum clearance project was officially sanctioned to forcibly move the poor population to the WEA. But three years later, in 1927, it was reported that there was now a population of 15,000 displaced poor people in the WEA living 'in much discomfort owing to lack of services'. In other words, one slum had given way to another through a planned process of displacement. Consequently, a northern expansion was recommended, beyond Civil Lines and across the Grand Trunk Road, on the outskirts of the old Sabzi Mandi. In spite of this, the government had to agree to sanctioning 10 lakh rupees in 1930 for providing basic services such as water and sanitation in the WEA (although as much as 23 lakh were required). As part of the planned process of urban development, several new roads had also been built into the new areas and each one of these showed good financial returns. But in the absence of other facilities, civic conditions continued to deteriorate so much that, in 1936, an ICS officer was specially appointed to go into the question of 'congestion in Delhi' and suggest appropriate measures.

URBAN SPRAWL

The recommendations of this officer eventually formed the basis for a further expansion of the city towards the Agricultural Institute (Pusa) in the west with adjacent industrial areas next to the railways. For this purpose, the Najafgarh jheel had to be drained and this was accomplished by digging a cut through the northern tip of the Ridge. In tandem, the Western Yamuna canal was filled up to the Andha Mughal bridge across the Sahibi river (now reborn as the Najafgarh nala once the jheel had been drained) on the pretext that the waters provided breeding grounds for the dreaded mosquito. This also enabled an expansion into the north through the new colonies of Shaktinagar and Roshanara Extension. These colonies were specially meant for the working poor, who had been evicted from 'evil slum areas' (as designated by the ICS officer) of the Walled City (now no longer with walls). Other areas from where the poor were displaced during the late 1930s were the Mohtaj Khana (destitute home) next to Sabzi Mandi, Rehgarpura (leather workers' hamlet) in the WEA (now reborn as genteel Karol Bagh), and Kala Pahar (black mountain) near Sarai Rohilla. The lands they vacated were converted gradually into middle-class residential areas.

The 1941 census revealed that, in forty years, the population had more than doubled to 9.17 lakh. The next few years were politically tumultuous and there was little time for mundane matters like town planning. But, with the partition of the country in 1948, there was a mass exodus from across the border and 4.5 lakh refugees arrived almost overnight in Delhi. The Ministry of Rehabilitation was entrusted with the task of resettling this huge population and it accomplished this by setting up a circle of colonies around the periphery of the city, mostly within the boundary set by what is now Inner Ring Road. Most of these 'refugee' colonies can be recognized by the names of the national leaders after whom they were named—Laxmi Nagar, Naoroji Nagar, Patel Nagar, Sarojini Nagar, Ranjit Nagar, and so on. The displaced families with means were rehoused in these colonies while others were allotted (mainly illegally) the large number of houses abandoned by those who had moved to Pakistan. Abandoned and new shops and industrial plots were also liberally made available for the refugee traders and entrepreneurs to economically and socially rehabilitate themselves.

However, this huge 'planned' expansion had its corollary effect on the city. In 1955 there was an epidemic of jaundice in the elite core of the city, in areas such as Civil Lines and New Delhi, and 700 people died. In the subsequent investigation it was discovered that considerable amounts of untreated sewage from some of the newly constructed planned refugee colonies at the periphery of the Ring Road were being discharged into the Najafgarh nala, which, in turn, was releasing its load into the Yamuna just downstream of the pumping station at Wazirabad. The city's water supply source was thus contaminated, resulting in the spread of the epidemic. In response to the disaster the Ministry of Health immediately set up a Town Planning Organization (TPO) and a barrage was constructed across the river at Wazirabad to separate the nala discharge from the water intake. The TPO also produced an Interim General Plan in 1957 to improve sanitation in the city by further displacing the poorer quarters, markets, and enterprises from the centre to the periphery, which is a good example of how the breakers of a city assume the mantle of makers, and reality is subsumed by myth.

IMPOSING ORDER

In order to provide better administrative and financial support to the planning exercise, Delhi was declared a Union Territory in 1956 and the Delhi Development Authority (DDA) was constituted in 1957 by an Act of Parliament 'to check the haphazard and unplanned growth of Delhi . . . with its sprawling residential colonies, without proper layouts and without the conveniences of life, and to promote and secure the development of Delhi according to plan'. For the next three years the TPO, guided by experts from the Ford Foundation, developed a Master Plan for Delhi for twenty years and this was presented along with maps and charts for unprecedented 'public' discussion in 1960, eliciting over 600 objections and suggestions from (as documented in the final Plan itself) 'the public, cooperative house-building societies, associations of industrialists, local bodies, and various Ministries and Departments of the Government of India'. It is interesting that associations of the working poor did not appear in this list of what constitutes the 'public'. An ad-hoc Board was appointed to go into all these objections and it reportedly granted a personal hearing to all the objectors. Eventually the Master Plan of Delhi was formally sanctioned in 1962 and came to be known as MPD-62.

MPD-62 acknowledged that Delhi was likely to have an urban population of 56 lakh by 1981 unless measures were taken to restrict it to 50 lakh (without, of course, stating why an extra 6 lakh could not be accommodated—as had happened perforce in 1948). The planners proposed to do this by building a 0.6 km wide green belt around Delhi and diverting the surplus population to the seven ring towns in Uttar Pradesh and Haryana. In a repetition of colonial history, it was once again decided that the Walled City would be 'thinned out' by relocating the population to New Delhi and Civil Lines. In 1961 there were also estimated to be 8,000 industrial units, which were located in 'non-conforming' industrial areas such as Karol Bagh, Shahdara, Naraina, Malaviya Nagar, Kalkaji, Tilak Nagar etc. So, several new industrial areas were designated for accommodating these industries on 5800 acres. The plan also provided for 85 square yard plots with services for poorer families who were going to come to Delhi to work in these industrial areas and commercial centres to be set up in different zones. In the process the DDA became the sole developer of the largest nationalization of land in the world, outside the Communist nations.

But by 1971 it was becoming clear that the city was going to grow far beyond the calculations (but not the declared targets given in the Master Plan) of the planners. The number of industries had increased to 26,000 and there was a huge spurt in the squatter population of the urban working poor—although both these had been anticipated by the Master Plan. So, in a frenetic burst of activity, the administrative machinery swung into action and, from 1975 to 1977, 1.5 lakh squatter families, consisting of a total population of 8–9 lakh were forcibly moved out of the centre of the city into resettlement colonies on the periphery of the growing city. Each family was entitled to a plot of only 25 square yards with common services of water, electricity and sanitation, and 60,000 such plots were demarcated, mainly on the low-lying Yamuna flood plain to the east. Interestingly, all the colonies were located very near the new industrial areas, thus indirectly giving a clue about the working class character of the evicted population required for providing cheap wage labour. At the same time, in 1977, the government regularized 567 'unauthorized' colonies which had come up in contravention of the Master Plan, inhabited by a more white-collar population, so that they could now officially avail basic civic services that had been denied them earlier because they were unauthorized.

MODIFYING PLANS

A new Master Plan should have been ready by 1982. But, instead, the entire city was geared to host the Asian Games that year. Numerous roads, hotels, flyovers, offices, apartments, and colonies were constructed to cater to the needs of the Games and the anticipated commercial spillover. The second Outer Ring Road became a magnet for further commercial and residential development. So while one work force was moved out of the city during the 1975–77 period to make space for the infrastructure required for the Games, another had to be summoned for building the new infrastructure between 1979 and 1982. It is estimated that 10 lakh workers came to Delhi during this period alone. But the city fathers claimed that they could not cope with this additional 'burden'. In 1985, the National Capital Region Board was set up in an attempt to plan for the balanced growth of the extended region around the capital where this 'surplus' population would be accommodated.

Also in 1985, the first draft of the second Master Plan was published for comments. However, unlike the first Plan, this one was not summarized or translated into Hindi and Urdu, nor was it distributed publicly. Nevertheless, the draft came in for severe criticism from the government itself as being 'conceptually defective' and the Delhi Urban Arts Commission (DUAC) was asked to prepare another plan. DUAC took a close look at the failures of the first Master Plan to detail its own Conceptual Plan. It was discussed in a select committee and modified to yield the second Master Plan, known as DMP-2001. This plan, probably recognizing the failure of the government to meet the targets set in MPD-62, lowered the bar and called for limiting the urban population (to 112 lakh) by de-industrialization (in other words, rendering the labouring classes redundant), though it had nothing to offer for the non-conforming industrial units already existing (then estimated at 24,000). Thus, on one hand the authorities grudgingly acknowledged the contribution of the working poor in making the city, but on the other hand the planners persisted in deliberately breaking their livelihoods and shelter. Interestingly, DMP-2001 displayed the modern planners' inherent ignorance of indigenous planning when it called for a 'special area' status for the Walled City as 'it cannot be developed on the basis of normal planning policies and controls'.

Two years after the sanction of the new Plan, in 1988, there was an outbreak of cholera reminiscent of the 1955 jaundice epidemic. This time, 1500 people died and they were all from the 44 resettlement colonies that had been constructed during 1975–77 and the 625 slum clusters where the working poor lived. These included areas like Gautampuri, Seelampur, Nand Nagari, Kalyanpuri, Dakshinpuri, and Mongolpuri. Unlike in 1955, however, there was no concerted response from the administration. Even the disbursement of compensation (which had been laid down as part of procedure during the jaundice epidemic of 1955) was withdrawn, though it was recognized that the disease had spread through ground water contaminated due to inadequate sanitation measures. This was inevitable given the nature of the low-lying areas in which the resettlement colonies had been located, by plan, in the first place. Thus, DMP-2001 was not only unable to tackle the problems created by the earlier period, it did not even incorporate its own analysis of the failures and weaknesses of past planning in its recommendations.

CITY AND CLASS

Today Delhi has spread far beyond the confines of the Outer Ring Road. The green belt, which was specified in MPD-62, has largely fallen victim to land developers. The resettlement colonies and industrial areas, that were supposed to be at the fringe of the city, have been drawn into its ambit. Narela, for instance, which was supposed to be a ring town under MPD-62, is now a connected suburb. Gurgaon, Faridabad, and Ghaziabad are contiguous urban sprawls and the arterial roads and national highways are the most congested in the region. Increasing numbers of the poor continue to live in shanty towns without services. In 2008 it was estimated that there were over 1500 unauthorized colonies without civic amenities, over 1100 slum clusters with minimal urban services, and as much as 60 per cent of the population lives in sub-standard housing because the civic authorities have been unable (or unwilling) to provide adequate space for the shelter and livelihoods of the very people who constitute the backbone of the city's economy. Once again, history as it unfolds repeats the question of who are the makers and who are the breakers of the city?

For such an ancient city, it is to be expected that history will provide some curious twists and lessons for the makers of the new city. But, as the vision of a world-class city rises over the social horizon, new history emerges to be even more formidable and gnarled than the old, as it refuses to acknowledge the presence of the working poor while catering only to the exclusivity of the elite. Even the courts appear to be colluding in this although their mandate is to preserve the balance between the classes. Thus, between 1994 and 2002, thirty manufacturers' and resident welfare associations filed writs in the Delhi High Court praying for the removal of slum encroachments from their areas, while thirty-six slum associations and individuals filed petitions asking for adequate housing. But, by November 2002, without giving any opportunity to the slum dwellers to be heard, the judges of the two Benches hearing the various cases, ordered the demolition of all slums as well as quashed the policy providing for resettlement of those who were evicted. In this manner, two judgements by two judges gave sweeping powers to the administration to uproot slum dwellers everywhere in the city.

LAW AND JUSTICE

Subsequently, when one of the High Court judgements was temporarily stayed by the Supreme Court, that Bench on its own volition took up the issue of pollution of the Yamuna river and in March 2003 directed all concerned authorities 'to forthwith remove all the unauthorized structures, jhuggies, places of worship and/or any other structure which are unauthorizedly put (sic) in Yamuna Bed and its embankment'. But when the Uttar Pradesh Irrigation Department Employees Federation challenged the construction of the Akshardham temple on the same Yamuna riverbed, the Court held that the temple was an existing reality built at great cost, and dismissed the writ. In January 2004, a series of ruthless demolitions of unauthorized constructions began all over the city. It may thus be seen that there is a systematic exclusion on the one hand and selective inclusion on the other, that masks the ideological divide between who creates and who destroys the structural fabric of the city and for what purpose.

This bifocal view continues unashamedly. At august gatherings of the elite, speakers wax eloquent about Singapore and Paris and Shanghai. Eminent industrialists hobnob with high profile television commentators, senior bureaucrats, and the city's beautiful people to announce the coming of the global, shining future. When the designer malls on MG Road were partially brought down in early 2006 there was a huge hue and cry. The sealing and demolition of about 1000 shops and commercial establishments in the next few months occupied centre stage in all the newspapers and the Government was forced to introduce a Bill in Parliament to put an end to these. But there was little or no concern in the media for the over 60,000 poor working families uprooted in three years in the name of 'beautification' for the world class city. Many of these families have been sent to remote sites like Bawana and Sabda Ghevra for so-called 'resettlement', where the stark non-availability of basic facilities like toilets and transport, water and electricity, employment and education, dispensaries and dustbins have been systematically documented by voluntary groups. But whenever evidence of these appalling conditions has been placed before the superior courts and human rights bodies, they have been arrogantly brushed aside.

What is concealed behind this play of history is that both sets of lives across the class barrier are affected by the failure of inclusive governance in the city. Thus, only one-third of the housing stock, one-fifth of the commercial space, one-third of the industrial area, and one-sixth of the informal sector space targets, as stipulated by DMP-2001, have actually been made available in the city in the last 25 years by agencies such as the DDA and the Municipal Corporation of Delhi. Hence, the unfortunate citizens, whether those wishing to operate shops and services, or those struggling to survive on an inhospitable piece of land, have had no other choice than to become 'illegal', 'unauthorized', and 'non-conforming'. Within the network of relationships that encompass the city, between employer and employee, between service provider and consumer, between those who toil and those who soil, the inclusion of one is inevitably affected by the exclusion of the other. But, instead of recognizing this interdependency and holding the agencies to task for their failure, the Courts have victimised those who have tried to create economically viable alternatives in housing and employment through their own enterprise and imagination.

In the meantime, the executive merrily continues to invest huge amounts of public money in projects like the Metro, the Commonwealth Games, and the vast residential and shopping complexes in the south and east of the city.

DYING LIGHT

In effect, the rulers of the city have ignored the fundamental principles of science (what causes pollution?), justice (who is accountable?), and human rights (men and women are to be treated equally?) to deny the urban poor their entitlements while favouring the affluent. This has been further complicated by the fact that the Constitution recognizes only those persons as 'citizens' who either have a birth certificate or hold a title to property. In a country where the majority of births go undocumented and at least one-third of the population has no property, such a definition of citizenship is farcical. It completely disempowers those who labour for a living but have no papers to prove that they exist in the eyes of the law. It gives enormous leeway to the police, municipal, and sundry other officials to harass and extort from all those who have no written proof of citizenship. But will the bricklayers and stonemasons vanish to suit the vision of the masters? What about the pullers and the loaders, the nannies and the drivers, the repairmen and saleswomen? What about the waste pickers and sewer cleaners, the delivery boys and tailoring girls, the factory workers and the artisans? Do they not make the city as well? And what do they get in return? Those who service the city get no services in exchange. And yet they are regarded as thieves and pickpockets, a burden on the city and creators of dirt. Over them hangs the perpetual threat of 'illegality' and 'demolition'.

SIMMER OF DISCONTENT

The pages of contemporary history are once again echoing an oft repeated question: will the working poor go silently into the night? Or will they rage, rage against the dying of the light? Whatever evidence is coming, through the eyes of those involved in a dialogue with them, indicates that there is vast discontent brewing within the army of the dispossessed. The rag picker on the streets, the watchman outside the bungalow gates, the ayah who cleans and dusts and sweeps within, the driver and the electrician and the plumber and the mason who drift in and out between outer and inner spaces, watch how the rich play at both work and home. They hear the voices of arrogance that claim the city for their own. And when they return to their homes in the midst of squalor and want, they also know that Delhi is being transformed into Paris.

On one side there are the visual and audio images of Radio Mirchi; the gleam of shop windows and ice-cream parlours; the sophisticated voices of *bhaav* and *sanskriti*; the smug seminar satisfaction of 'problem-identified, problem-tackled, problem-solved'; the seductive calls to drink more water for healthy skins; the invocation of Las Vegas and Singapore and Sydney as the icons for modernity; and the vacuous assertions of the cheer-leaders that 'we can do it'. On the other side are the slapping sounds of naked feet on the road pulling cartloads of goods; nimble fingers deftly cooking rotis for shrinking bellies; the struggle to get children into petty government schools where they will be called offspring of bhangis; the daily search for shreds of dignity within the violence of the public latrines, the packed buses, and the policed streets.

In between there is also the pause for reflection; the nagging question—is this the city we really want? But, curiously enough, this pause finds no space in the conference halls of the effete. The captains of industry and commerce, the suave TV anchor, the omnipotent bureaucrat-administrator, the hip-hop college student, the outstanding engineer, are all convinced of their place in destiny as the makers of the future. But for that they have to inevitably break the past—and, often, the present too. So as the Metro glides through the city the commuters are unaware of the huge cost the city is paying for this symbol of modernity, and of the thousands whose homes and livelihoods were removed to make way for the steel rails. The sportsmen and tourists who streamed into the city in 2010 were not told that their games are to be played on the graveyards of labourers who constructed the stadia and hotels and were then banished into the wilderness.

MAKING CHOICES

The question is whom do we choose to believe? Do we trust those 6 lakh families who live in the *pucca* colonies of the city? Or do we listen to those voices from the 6 lakh families located in the jhuggis? What about the 7 lakh in the *kachchi* colonies? And the 4 lakh who have been forcibly moved from one arena of illegality into another to inhabit the resettlement areas? And do we completely forget the two lakh now condemned to inhabit the pavements because there is no affordable space for them anywhere? Every third human being in Delhi is part of the workforce, those who sustain the life of the city, and 80 per cent of them are in the informal sector. So whom do we believe? The officials of the Confederation of Indian Industry gloating over 8 per cent–plus growth, or the workman shading his eyes from the hot afternoon sun, '*Dilli mein mazdoor ke liye kuchh nahi hai, kuchh nahi hai*' (There is nothing in Delhi for the labourer, nothing)?

The way forward depends upon the choice we make. If we believe the property developer, the expert, the bureaucrat, the entrepreneur, and the politician, then we have placed our faith in those who are breaking the city but pretend to make it. If we open our minds to the sounds of the vegetable sellers and auto drivers, the brick-layers and beauty parlour assistants, the steel welders and sewer workers, the domestic bais and home-based *biri* producers, then we will hear the cadences of the actual makers of the city, but who are often accused of breaking it. Will the choice be made freely and democratically? Or will it eventually be made through the violence of another democracy being born on the streets? That too is a choice we may be forced to make—or break.

This article by Dunu Roy first appeared in Celebrating Delhi, *published by Penguin Books in 2011, ISBN 9780670084821.*

FACTS & MAPS

DELHI AT A GLANCE

DELHI AT A GLANCE

Description	Total	Urban	Rural
Area (in sq. km)	1,483	1,114	369
Population	16,753,235	16,333,916	41,9319
Males	8,976,410	8,749,410	227,000
Females	7,776,825	7,584,506	192,319
Population (0–6 age group)	1,970,510	1,914,737	55,773
Males	1,055,735	1,024,900	30,835
Females	914,775	889,837	24,938
Decennial Population (%) (1991–2001)	20.96%	26.56%	55.61%
Literacy Rate (%)	86.34%	86.43%	82.67%
Density of Population (in sq. km)	11,297	14,667	1,135
Sex Ratio (females per 1000 males)	866	867	847

DELHI POPULATION

Year	Total	Urban	Rural
1961	2,658,612	2,359,408	299,204
1971	4,065,698	3,647,023	418,675
1981	6,220,406	5,768,200	452,206
1991	9,420,644	8,471,625	949,019
2001	13,850,507	12,905,780	944,727
2011	16,753,235	16,333,916	419,319

DENSITY OF POPULATION IN DELHI (PERSONS PER SQ. KM)

Year	Delhi	Urban	Rural
1961	1,792	7,225	258
1971	2,738	8,172	403
1981	4,194	9,745	507
1991	6,352	12,361	1,190
2001	9,340	13,957	1,692
2011	11,297	14,667	1,135

AREA OF URBAN & RURAL DELHI DURING 1961–2011 (IN SQ. KM)

Year	Total	Urban	Rural
1961	1,485	327	1,158
1971	1,485	446	1,039
1981	1,483	592	893
1991	1,483	685	798
2001	1,483	925	558
2011	1,483	1,114	369

NO. OF REGISTERED MOTOR VEHICLES

Year	Cars & Jeeps	M. Cycles Scooters	Auto rickshaw	Taxis	Buses	Goods vehicles	Total
1991	383,610	1,191,186	62,007	10,026	18,651	99,078	1,764,558
2001	968,894	2,265,955	86,985	20,628	47,578	161,650	3,551,690
2011	2,343,113	4,644,146	88,197	69,780	64,033	228,886	7,438,155

NO. OF HOUSES, HOUSEHOLDS AND THEIR AMENITIES

Item	1991	2001	2011
Number of Census Houses	2,446,143	3,379,956	4,605,555
Urban	2,209,620	3,135,268	4,481,133
Rural	236,523	244,688	124,422
Number of Households	1,860,748	2,554,149	3,340,538
Urban	1,696,828	2,384,621	3,261,423
Rural	163,920	169,528	79,115
Households by no. of dwelling rooms			
Total	1,860,748	2,554,149	3,340,538
No exclusive rooms	2,958	22,043	43,813
One room	827,338	973,520	1,074,917
Two rooms	500,767	689,480	989,686
Three rooms	287,666	458,546	666,480
Four rooms	137,953	229,801	348,639
Five rooms	47,998	75,740	101,185
Six rooms & above	56,068	105,019	115,818
Electricity available	1,479,620	2,371,811	3,310,809
Toilet facility available	1,179,797	1,991,209	2,990,741
Drinking Water facility available	1,382,367	1,912,467	2,618,982

POWER AND WATER CONSUMPTION IN DELHI

	2001	2007	2011
Daily water consumption (x100.000 KL / Day)	9,296	10,976	12,789
Daily power consumption (MW)	2,879	4,030	5,028

Provisional Population Census 2011. Source: Statistical Abstract of Delhi 2012, Directorate of Economics and Statistics, Government of NCT of Delhi Provisional

THE WORST FIVE CAPITALS FOR AIR POLLUTION

Capital	PM 2.5	PM 10	Sources
Delhi, India	153	286	Coal-based energy generation, transportation emissions
Doha, Qatar	93	168	Construction, transportation emissions
Kabul, Afghanistan	86	260	Dust from roads, transportation emissions, plastic, used motor oil, tires as source of fuel
Dhaka, Bangladesh	86	180	Brick kilns, construction and industrial sites, dust from roads, transportation emissions
Ulaanbaatar, Mongolia	68	148	Ash and emissions from coal stoves, coal-based energy generation, dust from the desert, unpaved roads and open soil surfaces, transportation emissions

Source: WHO, reports

NEW DELHI
CITY FUNCTIONS
2011

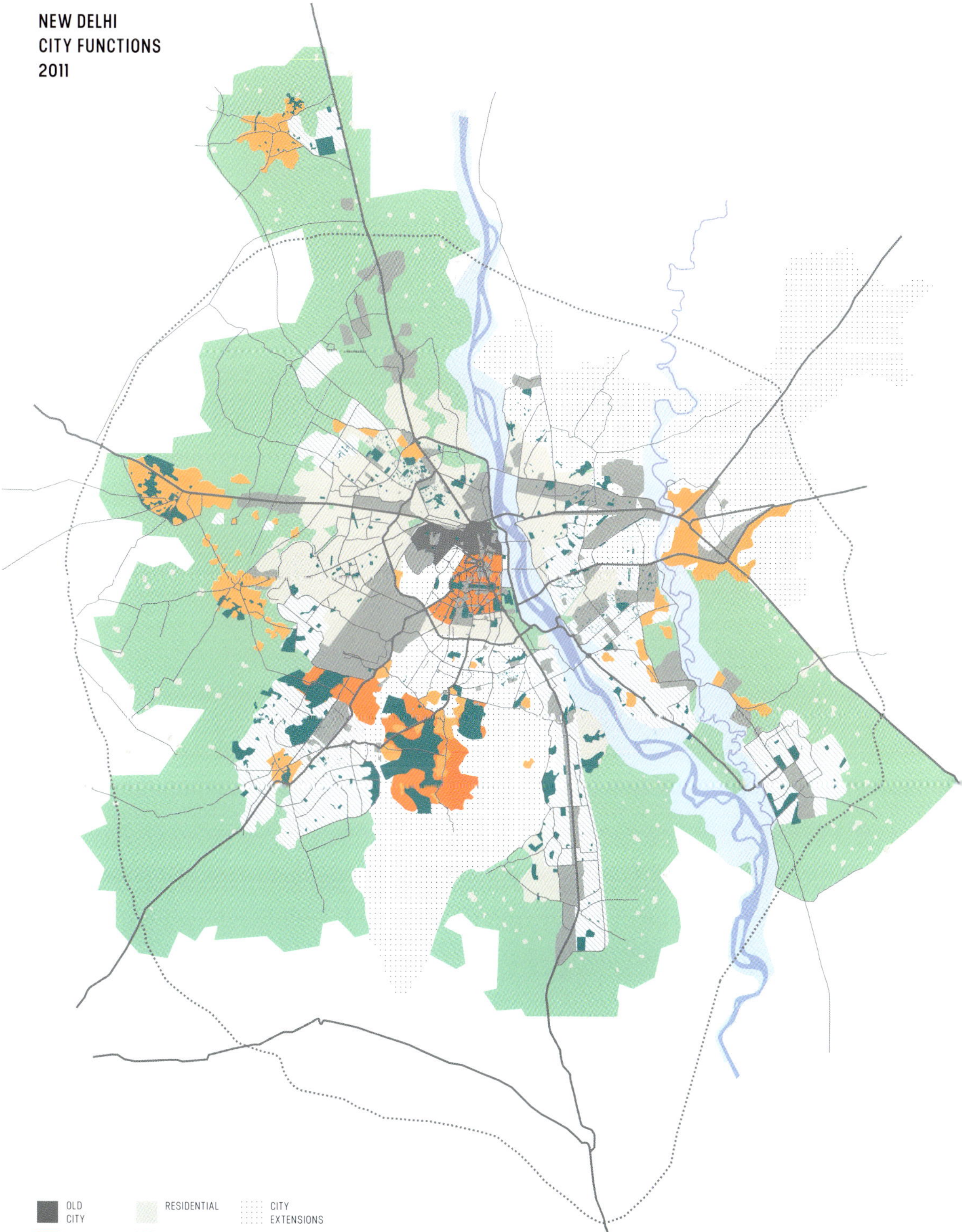

OLD CITY | RESIDENTIAL | CITY EXTENSIONS
LUTYENS | NON-RESIDENTIAL | GREENFIELD DEVELOPMENT | RIVER
VILLAGES | GREEN TOP | GREEN AREA | FLOOD PLAINS

0 5 10KM

NEW DELHI
CITY DEVELOPMENT
1857

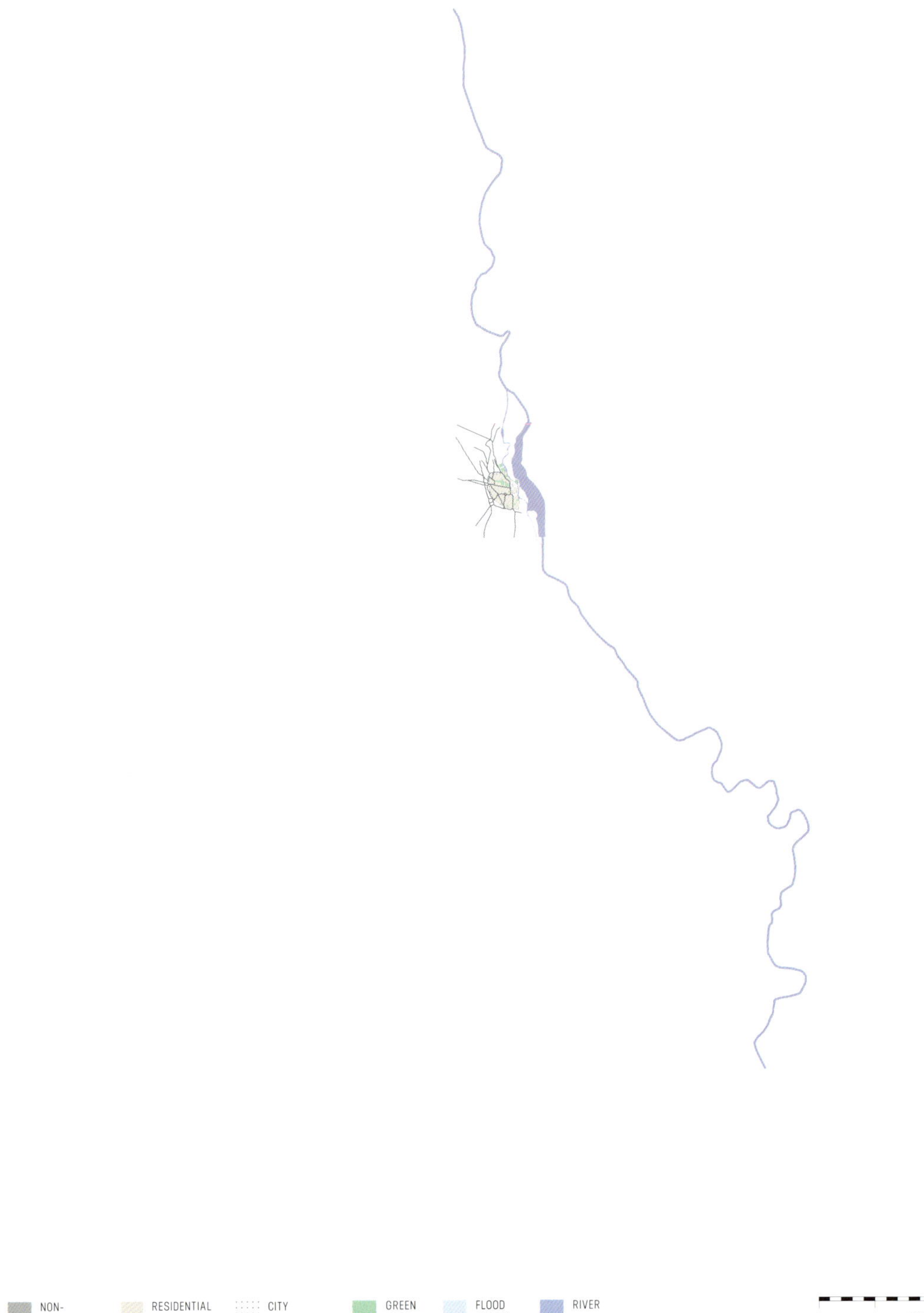

NEW DELHI
CITY DEVELOPMENT
1912

NON-RESIDENTIAL | RESIDENTIAL | CITY EXTENSIONS | GREEN AREA | FLOOD PLAINS | RIVER

0 5 10KM

NEW DELHI
CITY DEVELOPMENT
1962

NEW DELHI
CITY DEVELOPMENT
2001

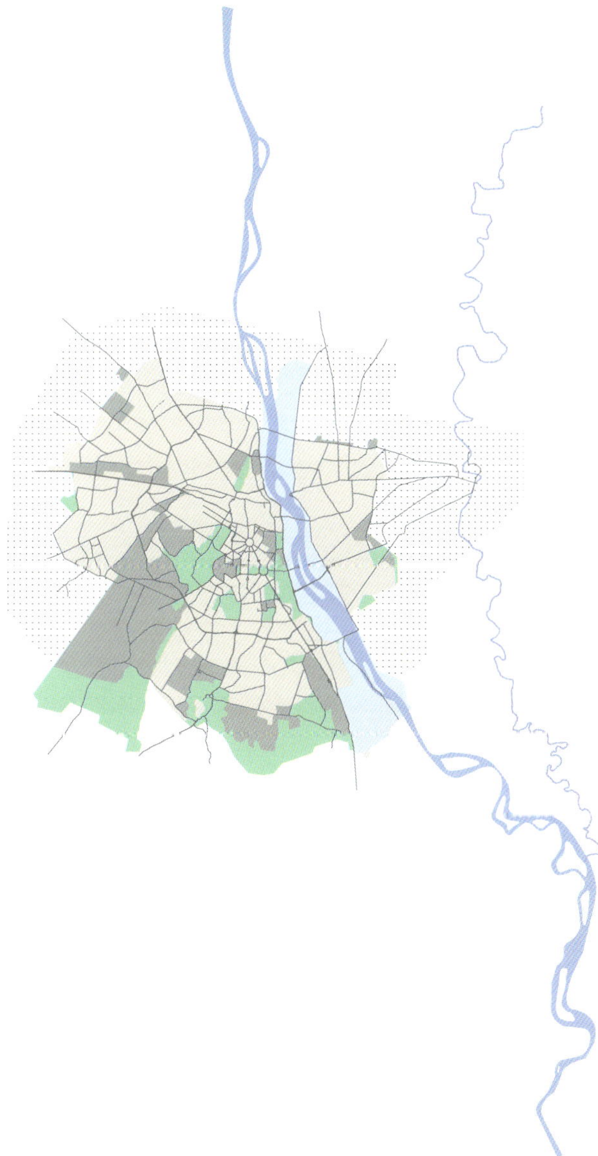

NEW DELHI
CITY DEVELOPMENT
2011

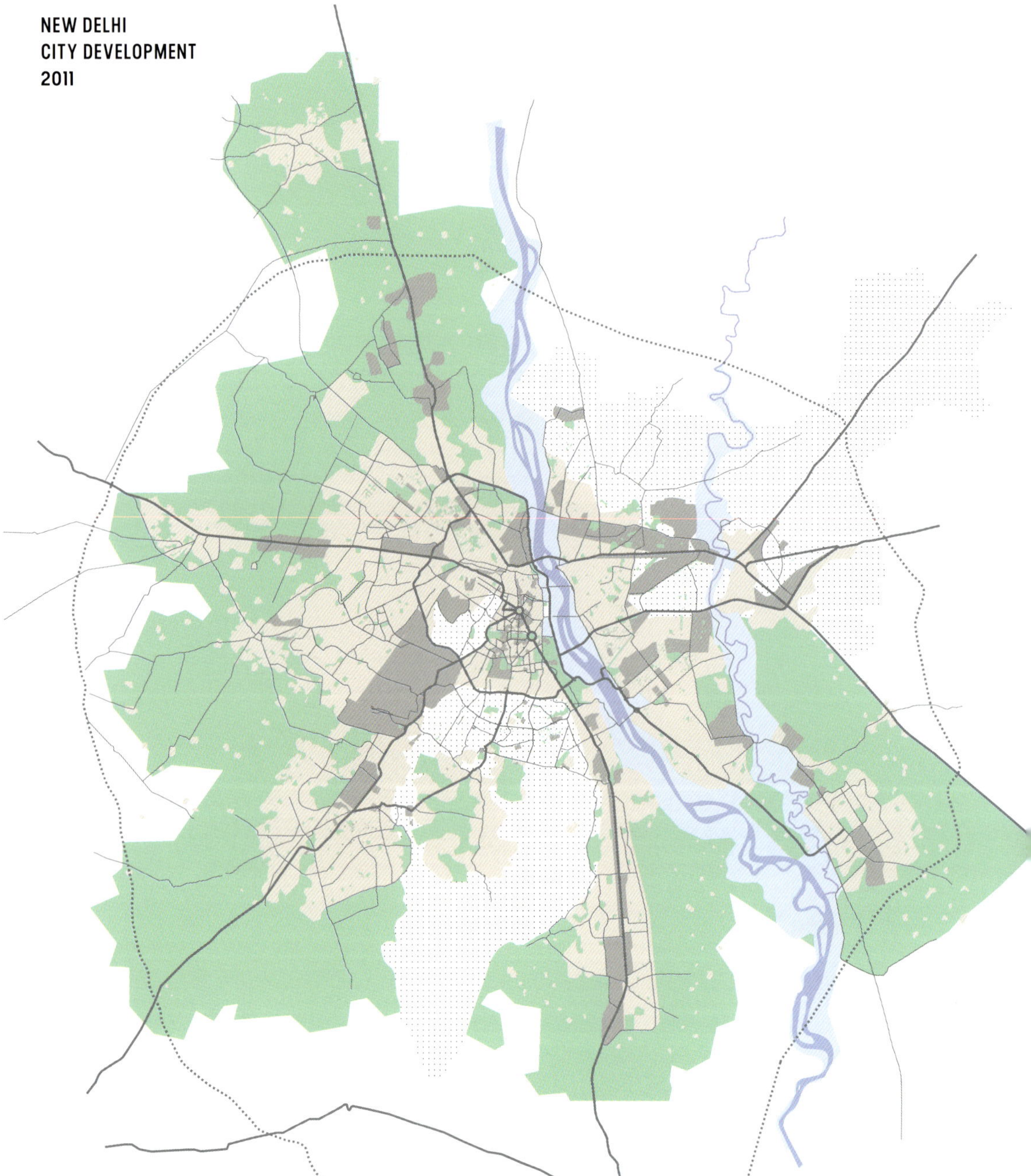

NEW DELHI
CITY DEVELOPMENT
2021

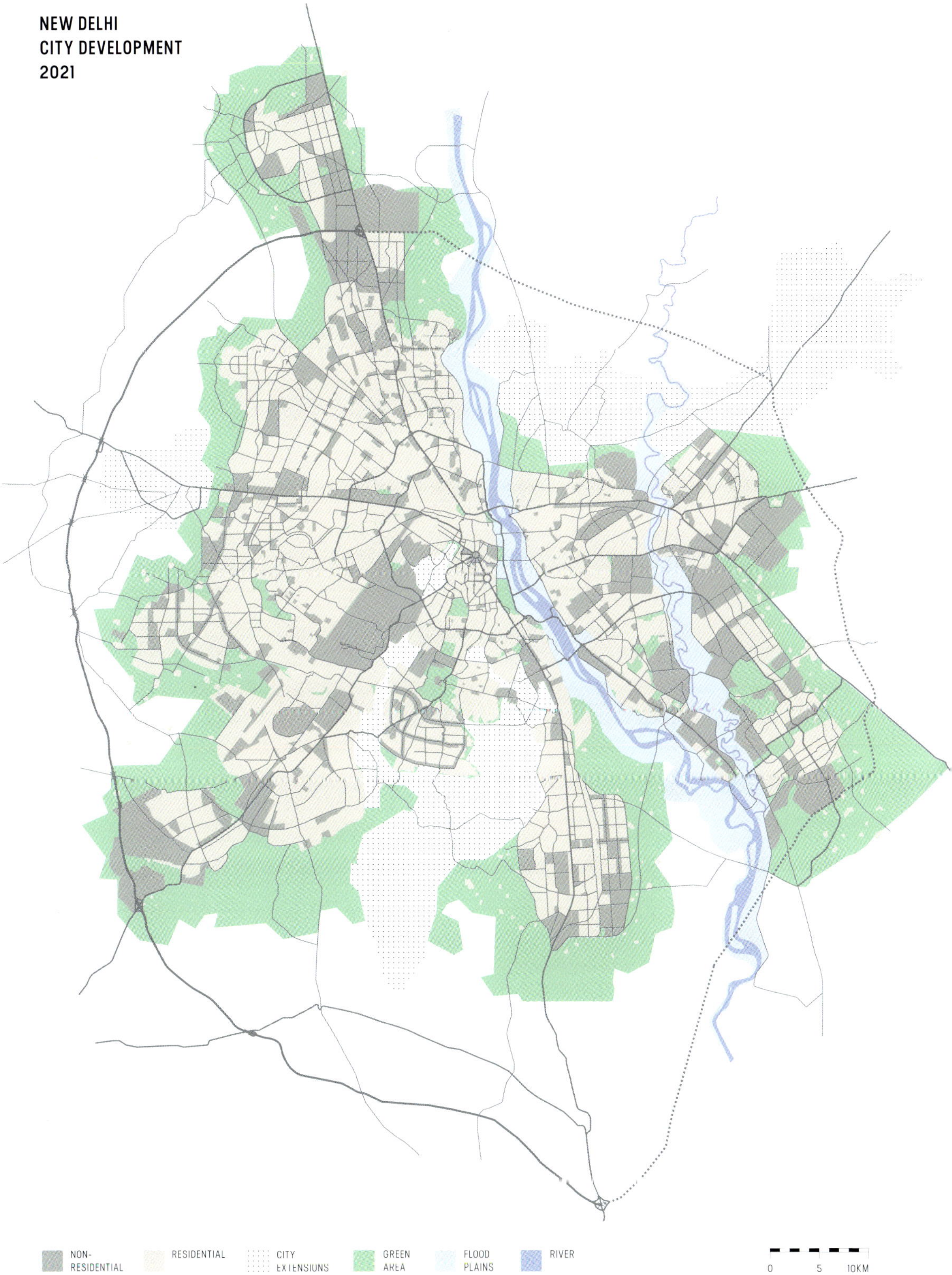

NEW NEEMRANA

ASHOK BHALOTRA

Ashok Bhalotra (1943) studied Architecture in Delhi and received practical training from members of Team X, the group of architects who, from the mid 1950s on, had challenged the doctrinaire approach of the Congrès Internationaux d'Architecture Moderne. He worked in India and Kuwait, and later in Paris at Woods & Candalis, as well as for Anatole Kopp.

From 1971 onwards he was attached to KuiperCompagnons, a firm based in Rotterdam, specialized in urban planning, architecture, and landscape. For Bhalotra, city plans and building types present a rich pattern of diversity and contradictions: pleasure and functionality, symbols and rituals, tradition and modernity, the sublime and the banal, order and chaos, reality and dream–all couched in the dialectic of dwelling and travel.

In late 2009 Bhalotra became the founder and director of FEWS for More. Sustainability is the key word related to FEWS for More: not only sustainability in the field of energy and use of materials, but also in the social, natural, cultural, and economic fields. FEWS for More advocates food, energy, water, and shelter for everyone across the globe.

The Delhi-Mumbai Industrial Corridor (DMIC) is at present likely to be India's most ambitious infrastructure programme. The project entails the development of industrial zones spanning six states in India, as well as creating new industrial 'smart cities' where next-generation technologies are converged across infrastructure sectors. In addition to new cities, the programme envisages the development of infrastructure linkages, such as power plants, assured water supply, high capacity transportation, and logistics facilities, as well as softer interventions, including a skill development programme to aid employment of the local populace.

Conceived as a global manufacturing and trading hub, the corridor is expected to spur economic development in these regions and to help develop industries. Its promotors claim that the planned USD 100 billion investments in the corridor will double employment potential, triple industrial output, and quadruple exports from the region in five years. In the first phase seven new industrial cities are being developed.

The programme was conceptualized by the governments of India and Japan, with funding shared equally by the two countries.

Probably currently India's most ambitious infrastructure plan, the Delhi-Mumbai Industrial Corridor (DMIC) project entails the development of industrial zones spanning six states in India, as well as the creation of several new industrial 'smart cities'–cities where new technologies are converged across infrastructure sectors. Conceptualized, supported, and funded by the governments of India and Japan, the programme envisages the development of infrastructure linkages, such as power plants, assured water supply, high capacity transportation, and logistics facilities, as well as softer interventions, including a skill development programme to aid employment of the local populace. Conceived as a global manufacturing and trading hub, the almost 1500-kilometre-long corridor is expected to spur economic development in these regions and to help develop industries. Its promotors claim that the planned USD 100 billion investments in the corridor will 'double employment potential, triple industrial output, and quadruple exports from the region in five years'.

PLANNING FOR MILLIONS

In the first phase seven new industrial cities are being developed. One of the first master plans to be completed was designed by one of the Netherlands' best known architects and planners: Indian architect Ashok Bhalotra of KuiperCompagnons in association with Royal HaskoningDHV, Ecorys, Cushman & Wakefield. Bhalotra shares some of the thoughts behind the planning for New Neemrana: a plan for an area of 165 square kilometres and a city of more than one million people located in the Khushkhera-Behror-Neemrana Investment Region (KBNIR), 107 kilometres south of New Delhi.

'When the urban planners and designers of KuiperCompagnons visited the KBNIR for the first time, they were impressed by the beauty of the arid Rajasthan landscape. Endless agricultural fields, groups of trees, dramatic hill ranges, scattered villages and even the presence of a historical fort reflect the environmental, social and cultural assets of the region. After experiencing this environment, we wanted the existing context of this area to play an important role in the development of our new metropolis for a million or more inhabitants.'

CITIES WITH HEART AND SOUL

Their appreciation of and sensitivity to the pre-existing cultural, geographical and urban context was in line with the vision of the planning team on what a city is and should be. 'In many rapidly urbanizing areas, large-scale developments have given limited attention to the local context. Too often this resulted in modern areas that lack "heart and soul".' And this although 'cities are the mirrors of society, reflecting the state of its culture, the economy, social relations, human values and, above all, the care for the environment and the climate. When one listens carefully, the city narrates the dreams, aspirations, fears and struggles of its inhabitants.' Keeping their first impressions of the region and their vision on cities in mind, Bhalotra and his team chose a different approach for New Neemrana. 'Besides providing for basic needs such as food, energy, water, and shelter, a city should give its people a sense of being at home.' 'People feel comfortable when they can identify themselves

FACT SHEET

CLIENT
Delhi-Mumbai Industrial Development Corporation Ltd.

CONSULTANTS
KuiperCompagnons (lead consultant), in association with Royal HaskoningDHV, Ecorys, Cushman & Wakefield

START OF PROJECT
2010 Notification Master Plan: 2013

DEVELOPMENT PLAN AREA
550 sq. kms

MASTER PLAN AREA
165 sq. kms

PROJECTED POPULATION
1.5 million (2040)

PROJECTED EMPLOYMENT
537,000 persons (excluding agriculture)

MAIN PROJECTED LAND USES
Knowledge, Residential, High-tech Industry, High-tech Agriculture

PROJECTED DWELLINGS
345,000 units

PROJECTED WATER DEMAND
380 MLD (2040)

RAIN HARVESTING
Mandatory for all land uses

PROJECTED ENERGY DEMAND
6,000 MW (2040)

SOLAR POWER
Minimum 25% of demand

ECOLOGICAL PROTECTION ZONES
6.5 sq. kms

SOLAR POWER
Minimum 25% of demand

EXISTING VILLAGES
42 (all integrated in Master Plan)

EXISTING POPULATION
65,000

with the local characteristics, when they are in an environment that they feel connected with.' Thus, 'the region's existing social, cultural, environmental and economic infrastructures were taken as a starting point.' The design embedded all natural and cultural assets, and most importantly no fewer than 42 existing villages. 'These villages are the place of significant informal social and economic infrastructures. We took great care to include them in the plan to ensure they will not be demolished and that new infrastructure, roads, and developments will pass alongside.'

RURAL REDEVELOPMENT AND URBAN DEVELOPMENT

The planners did more than just bypassing villages though. Bhalotra shared that his team took up the assignment as a combination of urban development and rural redevelopment. 'A key part of embedding the villages in the Master Plan concept is the inclusion of almost all existing local roads and tracks between villages.' 'We recognized that these roads and tracks are routes of habit, which have been used for generations. These routes form a fine layer at the local scale below the formal traffic circulation plan and add an extra dimension to the urban fabric. They also perform an important role in the landscape design concept, by becoming primary leisure and nature routes. Although retaining a limited vehicular function, these routes should be safe for all forms of non-vehicular traffic.'

GREEN CITY

In addition to making it a 'Smart City', Bhalotra also strived to plan New Neemrana as a 'Green City'. 'Special attention has been given to provide sufficient food, energy, water, and shelter for all the people in the new city in a sustainable manner. The region's most fertile grounds have been integrated into the Master Plan for high-yield multi-cropping agriculture. These high-tech agriculture grounds are located inside or in the close vicinity of the New City, therefore decreasing the negative effects of long-distance food-travel. Energy will be largely harvested from the abundant sun of Rajasthan. The Master Plan regulates that a minimum of 20% of all roofs must be covered with solar panels. This is in addition to the solar plants in the city. Finally, water will be harvested, re-used and recycled. This will significantly reduce the demand for water and only water-efficient (high-tech) industries will be allowed. In addition, areas are reserved for water infiltration during the monsoon period and existing water ponds and vegetation is maintained.'

In sum, New Neemrana will not just encompass a smart city, but will have a city that is 'rooted in the local identity, grows organically from the existing context and aims to offer a clean environment and fresh food in a compact and integrated urban environment.'

This article is based on the essay 'Moulding the Region to a New City', which first appeared in the July-September 2014 issue of the magazine My Livable City.

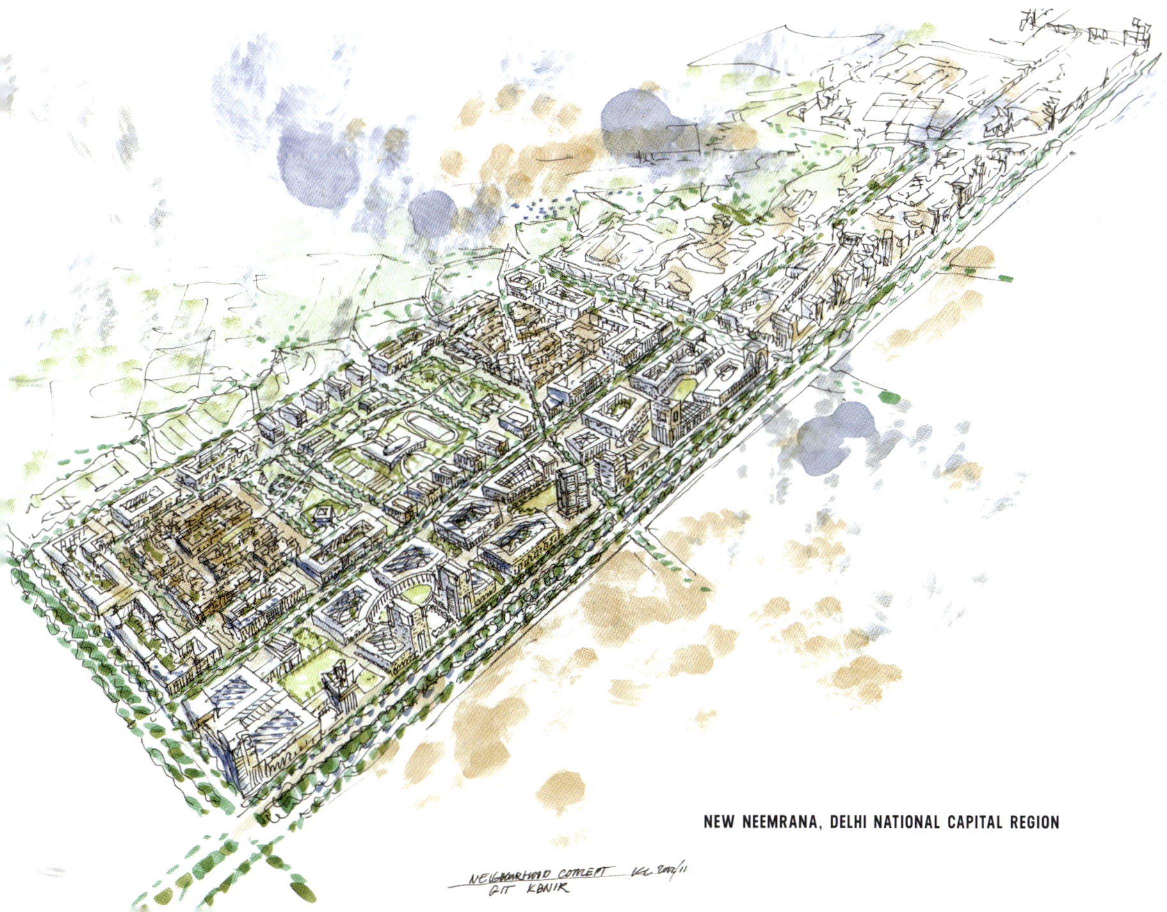

NEW NEEMRANA, DELHI NATIONAL CAPITAL REGION

A TRIBUTE TO JOSEPH ALLEN STEIN

SHYAM KHANDEKAR

Shyam Khandekar (1951) studied Architecture at IIT Kharagpur and pursued postgraduate studies in Planning and Building in the Netherlands, and Urban Design 'with a cocktail of landscape architecture' in the United Kingdom. He worked at various architecture and design firms in India and Europe, before starting his own practice, Khandekar: Urban Design and Landscape, in 1988 in the Netherlands. In 2008 his firm merged with BDP, to become BDP Khandekar. His expertise as an architect is combining essential aspects of urban design, landscape architecture, and infrastructure in projects. He has also lectured extensively on liveable cities.

Khandekar has won international awards with two of his housing and urban regeneration projects in the Netherlands (i.e. Monnikenhuizen in Arnhem and Paleiskwartier in Den Bosch) and received wide acclaim for his plans for regenerating the historic town of Coevorden. Nirlon Knowledge Park, his first Indian project, won the International Property Award 2012–Asia Pacific Region. Presently he is leading the design team for a sustainable new IIT campus in Jodhpur, India.

I had the good fortune of working for Joseph Allen Stein (1912–2001) in 1977–1978. I had just returned to India after completing postgraduate studies in the Netherlands and England. It was a time of limited opportunities in India for young designers like me. What most young architects then aspired to was a job at the studio of one of the celebrity architects. Charles Correa in Mumbai and Achyut Kanvinde and Raj Rewal (then still with Kuldip Singh) in Delhi were on the top of their list.

My aspirations were different. In my five years since graduation, I had already discovered that architecture, when limited to designing only the building, was irrelevant to making our cities more liveable. I wanted to work for a practice where architecture was embedded in its larger context: in landscape and history. So, one morning in Delhi I went to Joseph Stein's office in Sunder Nagar–my ambition neatly folded between my drawings in my portfolio. He offered me a job. I became part of a team of young designers who all had then just recently joined the practice. My compatriots were Ashok Lall, Revathi Kamath, and Rommel Mehta, who have all since made their mark on the design profession in Delhi.

JOSEPH ALLEN STEIN

Joseph Allen Stein was born in 1912 in Omaha, Nebraska (USA). He studied Architecture at the University of Illinois, graduating with a Bachelor's degree in 1934. The same year, along with Eero Saarinen of Yale University, he was awarded the Medal of the Societe de Architectes Francais as an outstanding student in the 'beaux arts'. He went on to study at the Ecole des Beaux Arts de Fountainebleau in France, before returning to Illinois to get his Master's degree in Architecture.

In the years that followed he moved to California, where, among other things, he worked for the internationally renowned architect Richard Neutra. Then, in 1940, he set up his own practice in California. It was during his practice in California that Stein started seeing architecture beyond buildings, and became fascinated in designing the total environment.

TO NEWLY INDEPENDENT INDIA

A few years before landing in Delhi, Stein and his wife had left the USA disillusioned by the McCarthy era. Via Mexico and Italy, they arrived in India in 1952. Stein was recommended personally by his former employer, architect Richard Neutra, to head the department of Architecture and Planning at the Bengal Engineering College in Calcutta. In 1955 he moved to Delhi and started his practice there, first under his own name and soon as Stein, Doshi and Bhalla. For those working on design at the practice in Delhi, it essentially meant working with Stein though. Doshi was operating from Ahmedabad, and our meetings with Bhalla were limited to only business and financial issues.

From the start Stein was excited to be in India. His first years in India coincided with the first post-Independence years. He later related in an interview the optimistic mood that prevailed:
'It was a very stimulating extraordinarily interesting time. India was almost newly independent. It was like coming to the United States when Thomas Jefferson was alive. Something like that. Nehru was Prime Minister, who was an outstanding

man. He had his flaws–many great men are flawed, maybe all human beings are flawed. But he was an extraordinarily beautiful and intelligent man, and he cast an aura over India that was very attractive. At that time the memory of Gandhi and Tagore was fresh and bright in India, and had very much influence among the students. So students were very attractive people to work with ... they were idealistic and dedicated.'[1]

SUITABLE DESIGN

Stein's early years in India coincided with Le Corbusier's period in India (in connection with his assignment to design Chandigarh) and with Louis Kahn's assignment for the IIM Campus in Ahmedabad. But while both these high-profile international architects and their work had a great influence on the architects at that time in India, neither of the two made India their home. Stein, on the other hand, came to India, took time to understand it, to absorb its regionalism and to appreciate its landscape. He created an environment by his design which was eminently suitable to India; not by using a very bold architectural language which could be copied, but by designing his buildings with a subtlety so that they became part of their landscape. In fact it would seem as if they had always been there.

Possibly because of this design approach, and the resulting very subtle design vocabulary, those who learned from him were able to develop their own design language. This is in contrast to architects like Le Corbusier, who had a more imitable design dictionary, and whose design language was thus widely copied by students and professionals alike.

REGIONALISM

When I joined Stein's office he had just been awarded the design assignment for the Kashmir Conference Centre. What struck me most was his ability to design at several scales simultaneously. On the one hand, the site plans we drew extended across the Dal Lake to the hills beyond–anchoring the building in its surroundings. On the other hand, thoughts were being developed by Stein and his team on using local materials and colours to merge the building with its landscape. The regionalism in his design extended from the design of the landscape (influenced by Shalimar and Nishat Gardens) to the use of modified traditional craftsmanship and forms in the inlaid floors, wooden walls, and ceiling panelling of the interiors.

In the office I was impressed to see the talented team he had brought together at work. Seniors like Prithipal Singh, P. K. Chaudhery, S. B. Rai, J. K. Jain, and P. K. Madan had been with him for many years. Prithipal Singh in particular was a master of construction details. He drew them by hand. This was the time when drawings were still made with 6B pencils and Rotring pens!

'STEINABAD'

Over a period of more than three decades Stein had a series of assignments in the area near the historic Lodhi Gardens. Starting with the India International

Centre (delivered in the 1960s) and Ford Foundation Headquarters (1970s), and ending with the most public of them all: the India Habitat Centre (1990s).

The result was a series of institutional complexes where Stein's mastery of designing the whole environment–and not just the building–is showcased. The India International Centre shows ample sensitivity to the adjacent Lodhi Gardens. But, as with the Kashmir Conference Center and many of his other works, what is once again most striking is the fact that his design repertoire extends all the way from the larger context of relationship with the Lodhi Gardens, to the smaller details of the modern interpretation of the historic jaali. He cultivated in this and the other complexes in the area a sort of modern regionalism in design which is unparalleled in the recent history of Delhi.

For his contributions to the architecture of Delhi, and India, Stein was awarded the Padma Shri, India's fourth highest civilian award, by the government of India in 1992. It is only befitting to this great designer that–in addition to awards, and a lane formally named after him–the entire area south of Lodhi Gardens is now often locally referred to as 'Steinabad'.

THOUGHTS AND LESSONS

In spite of his great achievements, compared with some of his contemporaries, Stein has remained less well-known. He was essentially a quiet man, almost shy; someone who did not advertise his own achievements. Because of this, and maybe because his practice folded after his demise, his lessons have gone somewhat forgotten. A comprehensive book on him by Stephen White, published in 1993[1], was a major attempt to bring change to this. In the book, White conveys Stein's thoughts as they were shared with him in a series of interviews. Instead of paraphrasing Stein's powerful words, let me share here ad verbatim some of what I found to be his most illuminating lessons.

On the relation between nature and architecture, Stein said:
'Architecture is not an industrial subject. I think it is basically where man comes into relationship with nature. Building after all is something that exists on the earth.' (...) 'The root of architecture is to understand nature–the rhythm, proportion which can be found in the study of a tree is a beginning. Originality will come when it is ready. Bucky Fuller once said, "When I do a thing, I only try to do it right, I never try to make it beautiful. But when I am finished, if it is not beautiful, I know I have done it wrong ... " and I think this is very important.'

On marrying functionalism and regionalism, Stein noted:
'In the end when an architect designs a building, he cannot do it on the basis of function alone. I think there is plenty of scope for both, for functionalism and regionalism. There is a wide variety of choice in architecture. When you have exhausted the functional requirements, there is still an area of discretion, and this is where sensitivity to and appropriate response to place comes in.'

On man's response to ecology, Stein said:
'Much of my life has been spent in the observation of increasing stresses. Today there are twice as many people in the world than the ecology of the world at present levels of technology can easily support. This does not mean that they cannot be supported, it simply means that it takes good management to support

[1] J.A. Stein in 1987 to Stephen White in an interview as quoted in: Stephen White (1993) Building in the Garden: The Architecture of Joseph Allen Stein in India and California. (Delhi, New York: Oxford University Press).

the many people now on the earth. Previously, people could live without good management, without too much conflict. Now we cannot live without conflict unless there is science and management. Whether we have the capacity for it, no one knows.' (...) 'If the world is to find a way of living with itself, obviously we are going to have to find a way to become more conscious of ecology. Certain things are too true to ignore for ever, and one of them is the question of ecological balance, of establishing a sustainable society.'

Stein's own favourite saying, as recalled by his son, was: 'The probabilities are awful, but the possibilities are marvellous.'[2] It shows him to have been a realist and optimist folded in one.

2 "The probabilities are awful, but the possibilities are marvelous" Joseph Allen Stein's favorite saying, as recalled by his son Ethan.

MOMENTS OF SIGNIFICANCE

One and half years after I joined the firm, I left India again to return to the Netherlands to pursue higher studies. Stein gave me a private farewell at 'his' India International Centre. If I were to make a list of moments of significance in my long career encompassing work in Europe and India, that day on the veranda of India International Centre would be there. That day I said goodbye to probably the best architect-planner-landscape designer India has had in the post-Independence period.

I was back at the same location earlier this year. While in a meeting in one of the rooms on the upper floors of the complex, I noticed that under the protection of the steel frame (that, like a jaali, offers protection from the extreme weather conditions in Delhi) there were two parrots courting. I couldn't help but think it was the ultimate ode to Stein's concern for the total environment.

NDIA HABITAT CENTRE, DELHI

INDIA HABITAT CENTRE, DELHI

IHC INFORMATION CENTRE

INDIA INTERNATIONAL CENTRE, DELHI

INDIA INTERNATIONAL CENTRE, DELHI

INTERVIEWS

INTERVIEWS
INTERVIEWS
INTERVIEWS
INTERVIEWS
INTERVIEWS
INTERVIEWS
INTERVIEWS
INTERVIEWS
INTERVIEWS
INTERVIEWS
INTERVIEWS

REINVENTING LUXURY

AMBRISH ARORA

Ambrish Arora (1973) started his working career as a boat designer, and then moved to Spatial Design, doing a variety of projects in hospitality, retail, the non-profit sector, museums, and cinema. He founded Lotus in 2002 with Sidhartha Talwar and Ankur Choksi.

Lotus is a multidisciplinary architecture and interior design practice. International recognition has come with, among others, winning the World Holiday Building of the Year award at the World Architecture Festival 2011, a grand Jury Prize at the Design for Asia Awards, and a nomination in the Aga Khan Awards cycle 2013.

Consisting of a team of forty members the firm's work is grounded on the principles of conscious design, an approach that celebrates local resources, cultural influences and a keen sensitivity to the impact of the project and process on all stakeholders.

Arora has lectured at various international design forums, and has served as visiting faculty and juror at design institutes across the country. He is a member of the CII National Design Committee, on the advisory board of the Ansal University and has been voted among the country's most influential architects / designers by Architectural Digest in 2014.

'He is not an architect. But he is a really good architect.' This is how a fellow architect introduced Ambrish Arora to us. On our very last day in Delhi we visit him at his studio in the South Delhi area of Lado Sarai to discover this description to be true in various ways. We meet a jack-of-all-trades without any formal architectural training who nevertheless practices architecture with gusto. An artist who–with his unconventional approach and fresh ideas–is redefining contemporary Indian architecture and interior design.

FAIRY TALE

Arora's life story reads like a fairy tale. At age 16 he left his native Delhi to study Marine Engineering in Bombay (now Mumbai). Before long he realized he was not in the right place. 'I don't think I can spend 5 years here', he said to his father over the phone, three months into the programme. 'I can't waste time doing things that I don't believe in.' His father told him to do what he pleased, but find his own way as he could not support him. What followed was a series of unlikely apprenticeships.

He first joined a motorcycle mechanic who 'worked across the street'. Then he was trained in computer hardware maintenance and visited offices as a maintenance mechanic for a few months. Next, his father, a naval architect, took him in as 'cheap labour' at his boatbuilding unit yard, a tiny business he had started after his retirement from the navy. Arora spent four years building boats. When the company stabilized and his role became more and more that of a manager, working with his hands started to take a back seat. It was time for another change.

HABITAT CENTRE

On the lookout for a new adventure, Arora returned to Delhi. It was around the same time the now iconic Habitat Centre was in the making. Arora secured an apprenticeship at the firm responsible for designing some of the interiors, Oriole Design. He was thrown in the deep end. He took to doing whatever jobs were going in the studio and others did not want to do. 'Even though I had never designed furniture I was drawing up working details. Somehow my work experience allowed me to understand what I needed to do and I got familiar with it very quickly.' Laughing, he adds: 'They thought I was crazy though, because I did things like drawing items full scale on huge sheets of paper, showing every bolt, washer and nut and even the threading on the bolt!'

His commitment was rewarded. He made it from apprentice to partner in a year's time. Soon after he partnered with his mentor, Amardeep Behl, to start Design Habit. They worked on diverse projects including consultancy to the National Institute of Design for the interiors of the Khalsa Heritage Museum by Moshe Safdie and for Rajiv Sethi on the Basic Needs Pavilion at the World Expo 2000.

A new challenge came when friends of his business partner needed help in the art department of an art-house film produced by the German production company Pandora Film. Soon he took over production management of the said film, and when the project was completed stayed on to work as line producer on one more feature film, *Samsara*. Yet, he did not find his calling in cinema. He wanted to return to design, do something with his interest in more permanent spaces and the next logical step was to start, together with two of his colleagues from Design Habit, his own firm, Studio Lotus.

CAN-DO ATTITUDE

Although Arora calls himself 'plain lucky', it is not just good fortune that accompanied him on his journey. His father had a hands-on can-do attitude that he adopted and which has served him well, Arora says. 'If something was not working, my father would open it up. He told me not to be intimidated by objects, as everything is made by somebody. Every object has been thought through by somebody, and if I would open it, I would find out how it works and how it can be fixed.' This attitude is what makes him, in his own words, 'the fool who jumps in where angels fear to tread'. 'I am ignorant', he says laughing. 'So I don't have the fear of doing anything stupid. I do it and I accept that sometimes it works and sometimes it doesn't.'

When it came to architecture it did not just work, it became a great success. Twelve years after he started the firm, his Studio Lotus is now run by three partners and two associates, and employs a team of some forty-five people. It has been showered with national and international awards.

REDEFINING LUXURY WITH 10,000 SCISSORS

Among the projects that showcase the creative qualities of Ambrish Arora and his team are the retail spaces they designed in Delhi's luxury Emporio Mall. Several fashion designers came to Arora saying they wanted to create the same quality and luxury appeal for their shop as their high-end neighbours in the mall, such as Louis Vuitton, Dior, and Gucci. However, they only had a fraction of the budget of those big brands. Arora told them that what they needed was not a cheap copy of their neighbours' interior, but to redefine altogether what luxury meant.

'We made each of them look at their brand and say what defined them. One of them, Rajesh Pratap Singh was a very humble kind of guy who said: "I'm actually a high-end tailor. Just give me a white box, but let it tell a story."'

'Rajesh's work is about celebrating tailors and getting them to make beautifully crafted products. We created the concept of a shell within the shell of the building–a kind of lace box. The box would tell the story and would hold the clothes, while the engineering services would run outside it. We presented this to him and said: "We don't know what this box is going to be, but we want to work with something that has to do with your trade." Next, we started prototyping. One of our ideas was to deconstruct a sewing machine and reassemble its components for this box, but that did not work. In the end we came down to the very basics: scissors.'

'We got some 10,000 scissors and welded these together into big panels–the top and four sides of a box. From the outside, this construction we thus made looks like lace. Only when you come closer, you can see the scissors. All the work was done by hand in a workshop. We had made twelve patterns out of the same pairs of scissors and these came together as different stories for the ceiling, the sides, etcetera.'

'Do you know what the best part was? The cost for the entire shop was about 30 dollars per square foot! It cost nothing, as labour is so cheap and so were the materials we used. Yet, it is luxury: the interior is well designed and well made. It also captures the story of India where craftsmen can do amazing things against little cost. And it captures the story and spirit of the client, and his product.'

REINVENTING LUXURY IN JODHPUR

To date, Ambrish Arora's masterpiece is without doubt Raas Jodhpur: a luxury boutique hotel located in the heart of the old walled desert city of Jodhpur. Arora did the project in collaboration with Rajiv Majumdar from the Bangalore-based firm Praxis, under the name Lotus Praxis Initiative. 'A dream project', is what he calls it. It is also a project that earned Arora and his practice international recognition and several awards.

'To make it the success it is, we had to reinvent luxury again', he says. 'Almost all high end hotels in Rajasthan are either havelis, palaces, or are in some way aping the romance of old properties. They usually have a larger scale. We had a small site. Reinventing luxury was the only way to take on the competition.' It was achieved by optimizing the use of the available resources: the old structures present on the plot, the local materials and craftsmen, and the breath-taking view of the massive 15th century Mehrangarh Fort perched on top of a cliff overlooking the old quarter of the city filled with buildings painted blue.

OLD & NEW

Arora shows us his drawings and photographs taken at various stages of the project. 'There were four heritage buildings on the 6,000 square metre plot. These were built between the late 18th and mid-19th century. Through massing exercises we learned we could maintain the relationship of the four existing buildings the way we had found them and add the three new buildings we had in mind.'

The first old structure is a massive gate, a *pol*, through which you come onto a courtyard that now serves as the hotel's parking lot. At the opposite end of the yard stands a small new reception building. Behind that is the new main structure (with thirty-seven rooms and service areas), built as a wall obscuring the breath-taking view beyond; a view only revealed after walking 'through' the building into the next courtyard as if entering an arena, and upon opening the guestroom shutters. The second courtyard, behind the main building, houses the pool and a garden, and the remaining old structures. In one of them a spa was constructed, in another a restaurant.

'The work consisted of two parts', Arora says. 'One was restoration: scraping layers of paint, removing alien structures, and redoing limestone work; the other was making new buildings using the same techniques that were used for the old ones. For the restoration of the old buildings we didn't use cement; we didn't use steel. For the new buildings we used traditional scales and traditional materials juxtaposed with a contemporary construction framework. The great thing with India is that this is all still possible. And it's not very expensive either: all are living traditions.'

The result? Even though some buildings are brand-new, they are very much part of the old city. The top layer of the main new building merges with the surrounding blue structures. The lower layers respond to the pink sandstone buildings in the lower line of reference.

DOUBLE SKIN

What makes the new buildings truly unique, however, is that Arora and his partners adapted a local traditional element–the double skin–in a very creative manner. Arora explains: 'Around the entire building we created a double skin: we wrapped the building with sandstone slabs. These slabs came from a neighbouring quarry and were transported to the site on bullock carts.' The double skin facilitates natural ventilation. Only the guestrooms are air-conditioned. This is quite an achievement considering the fact that Jodhpur is located in the desert and has average summer temperatures of 41 degrees Celsius.

The double skin was fairly easily added on all sides except on the western façade of the building. There a solution needed to be found to unite two seemingly incompatible wishes: to have a heavy sandstone double skin and uninterrupted views of the fort from all balconies. 'To satisfy both wishes we needed to engineer something special,' Arora says. Which they did. They created an ingenious harmonica frame that allows 420-kilogram slabs of stone to fold open as smoothly as if they were curtains. It is designed so well that it not only performs the two functions it needed to, but even incorporates a third. It animates the western façade in a unique and very beautiful way.

PROCESS

Over the years Arora found that what matters most is the process. 'The entire design and construction process has to be collaborative, and with consideration for all who participate. If a client wants his buildings to be joyful, then it is important that every person who works on the building has joy doing so', he says. 'Ultimately it is really about finding purpose in what we are doing. We learned that we cannot have a joyful existence unless we find joy in what we are doing in our office day in day out and regardless of whether our designs get built or not.'

The philosophy that the end product should be the result of collaborative processes in all stages of the project has implications for the architect-client relationship. 'If for a project we decide we only want to work with local materials and local craftsmen, then crucial elements in the design might emerge from the way the materials and the people work on site', says Arora. 'As a result we might not be able to show an elevation [a detailed 3D presentation of the design] to the client before we start construction. Instead we ask clients to have faith in us, faith that we understand we are working on their luxury project and not our own activist project or so. Faith that we will honour our work, and their budget and time. Even if we can't show them immediately how we are going to do that.'

Faith, we are tempted to add, that Arora works the way he leads his life by letting the process, by letting what is actually happening, be his guide. Faith that–just like the fairy-tale story of his career from a college dropout to an award-winning architect–his projects will arrive at a more than happy ending.

RAJESH PRATAP SINGH, DELHI

RAJESH PRATAP

RAAS JODHPUR, VIEW OF THE HOTEL SET AGAINST THE MEHRANGARH FORT

COUTURIER GAURAV GUPTA'S FLAGSHIP RETAIL STORE, DELHI

PATIALA CRAFTS MELA, PATIALA, PUNJAB

MY DELHI
ABMBRISH ARORA

DELHI IS SPECIAL BECAUSE

Delhi is one of those cities that has moulded, shaped and reshaped itself over time to accommodate every kind of person.

MY FAVOURITE PLACE

I have been living with my eyes closed all this time. It is only now that I am discovering many places. The Mehrauli Archeological Park, for example. It is an old and crumbling area filled with historical structures and ruins from the Lodhi dynasty. The Jamali Kamali Mosque and Tombs located there are fabulous. So is the greenery, the parks. It is a really surprising and very beautiful place.

THE BEST PLACE TO RELAX

The various gardens, which Delhi has so many of.

MY FAVOURITE RESTAURANT

I prefer to eat at friends' homes and my own.

MY CHOICE OF TRANSPORTATION

I travel by car, but I use the metro and autorikshaws as well when I can. I would love to travel by motorcycle or bicycle (both of which I own), but Delhi is too polluted and crowded to make it safe to do so. During the week I travel by car mostly because I carry around lots of things with me all the time. My kids love going with the metro.

MY FAVOURITE LANDMARK

I don't have one. There are so many places in Delhi that I like. Lodhi Gardens, for example, and the Old Walled City too. But if friends would ask me where they should go during a Delhi visit, I would tell them to visit Mehrauli Archeological Park. There is a *baoli*, a stepwell, that has been restored beautifully and I would advise them to see. In fact, I like it so much that the picture of our team that we put on the website was taken there.

READY FOR DEMOLITION

I don't think anything should be demolished. Demolishing is such a waste. Things can and should be repurposed. I'm a strong believer in repurposing. It is there. Let us accept it. Just like we need to accept and love ourselves as we are, our strengths and our fallacies. So what needs to be changed is that people need to learn how to acknowledge the old and to integrate it in the new, rather than replace the old with something new. That is true sustainability.

MY FAVOURITE DELHI BOOK

Aaj Bhi Kharein Hain Talaab by Anupam Mishra of the Gandhi Peace Foundation. It is not about Delhi per se, but about indigenous systems of water management, and also about community building. I learned so much from it.

WHAT WE CAN LEARN FROM DELHI

Coexistence. We can learn how many different cultures can coexist, and how different time periods can coexist. You can go to certain pockets of this city and see people live the way people lived two hundred years ago, coexisting with people living with cutting edge technology.

MY WISH FOR DELHI

We, Delhi, or actually all of India, need to find our own way. Not because of nostalgia or because we want to maintain our tradition, but in order to stay relevant. Mahatma Gandhi said: 'God forbid that India should ever take to industrialism after the manner of the West. If an entire nation of 300 millions took to similar economic exploitation, it would strip the world bare like locusts.' A lot of people think of this as a negative statement. But to me, it is a very empowering statement. It says that we have to find our way. We can't use a fixed checklist that tells us how to do things; we need to create our own truth that celebrates our unique constraints and opportunities. A way that sets us free to be who we really are!

TRADITION AND MODERNITY

RAJ REWAL

Raj Rewal (1934) is one of India's best-known and most revered contemporary architects. He studied Architecture in Delhi and London. Subsequently he worked at the office of Michel Ecochard in Paris and taught at his alma mater (the School of Planning and Architecture in Delhi). In 1962 he also started his own practice, Raj Rewal Associates. He currently runs his office with a staff of about fourteen architects from a modest commercial building in South Delhi.

The receiver of many awards (among them the Gold Medal of the Indian Institute of Architects and the Robert Mathew Award of the Commonwealth Association of Architects, Chevalier des Arts et des Lettres of the French Government) and the subject of several monographs, 2013–2014 saw him honoured with an exhibition, at the Centre Pompidou in Paris, of his drawings and models, and photographs of his buildings.

Be it his Parliament Library, with their hand-crafted stone grills (jalis) and mandala shapes, his Asian Games Village whose morphology is inspired by traditional Rajasthan cities, be it his superbly climate-controlled education campus in Rohtak, where a series of courtyards provide the same shifting access as can be found in Fatehpur Sikri, or be it his Permanent Exhibition Complex in Delhi with its inbuilt sun breakers, Raj Rewal has excelled in creating buildings and complexes where sizing, structures, material use, and relation to the climate merge traditional architectural forms with the principles of modernism.

INSPIRATION

It was as a young lecturer at Delhi's School for Planning and Architecture in the 1960s that Raj Rewal revisited some of North India's architectural monuments. Accompanied by his wife, he drove from site to site, finding the inspiration he desired for his classes, and more. The building and construction techniques, the floor plans, and the materials he encountered at those monuments left a lasting impression on him as a budding architect.

'Particularly the cities of Fatehpur Sikri and Jaisalmer were such a surprise', Raj recalls these road trips. 'A surprise because I realized the structures and floor plans were old, yet they were also very modern. They are modern in the sense that their architecture is very rational; modern in the sense that the buildings respond perfectly to the climate they were built in. Fatehpur Sikri is also amazing because, even though it was constructed 450 years ago, it still holds one of the lightest structural systems in stone ever built in the world. In fact, these structures are more like contemporary reinforced concrete buildings than like masonry buildings. The walls are redundant and the loads are carried only on columns.' With a smile he adds: 'I remember thinking to myself, "Wow! Modernity already reached India so long ago".'

Around the same time that Raj was discovering the modernity of India's past, two major heroes of modernity, Le Corbusier and Louis Kahn, were putting their stamp on modern architecture in India. 'Of course I admired their work. I still like the poetry and print of it', Raj says. 'I admit it is almost impossible to compare their work with what was created in Fatehpur Sikri or Jaisalmer. But still, as a designer and architect I got more inspiration from the modernity of Fatehpur Sikri than that of either Le Corbusier or Kahn. It were these old cities that made me really understand how to work within the climate, what materials I should use, and how I should use these.'

CONCRETE INSTEAD OF STEEL

In 1962, after completing his studies in Delhi and London, and having spent a few years at the office of Michel Ecochard in Paris and a few years as a lecturer, Raj started his own practice in his hometown Delhi. He simply called it Raj Rewal Associates. His portfolio expanded quickly and now includes many iconic buildings. Up to the present day one very early project stands out for its pioneering modernity: the Permanent Exhibition Complex in Delhi.

The Hall of Nations, which is part of the complex, was India's first space frame structure, and it was, moreover, the world's first space frame structure made in concrete. When we ask how his plans were received, Raj shares that although he faced criticism he was positive from the start that it would be possible to replace the steel traditionally used for space frames with concrete. 'I had seen [the Italian engineer Pier Luigi] Nervi doing these concrete trusses', he says. 'I felt, if a truss can be done in concrete then why not this?'

Interestingly, Raj reveals that though it was one of his most daring innovations, there wasn't a grand idea behind his choice for concrete at the time. Instead, it was a rather pragmatic solution to a simple problem. 'The reason for choosing concrete was merely that we did not have enough steel in India for all the steel pipes and connections a space frame would require. India at the time was not an industrialized country. Therefore doing it in concrete was the only way we could make this design a reality.' Opting for concrete freed the available steel for use in other ways as well. 'I used steel inside and reduced the tension outside', Raj explains. 'It allowed us to put the stress, wherever it would be, on a concrete plate.'

POSSIBLE AND PREFERABLE

Although in the design stage the considerations regarding the choice of material were largely pragmatic, while working on the project the architect and his engineers soon learned that not only was it possible to do the space frame in concrete, it was actually preferable to using steel. 'Steel has limitations', Raj explains. 'You always have to take a steel tube, which is manufactured. You have to have a connection. A space frame has compression of side and tension members inside. You cannot change it in steel. That makes using steel actually the wrong way to build it.' He adds that he thinks his concrete space frame worked better than R. Buckminster Fuller's geodesic dome. 'Of course, Fuller got all the publicity of the world', Raj says, 'but I remember that when he came to India at the time, he was actually a little upset seeing my work. I had done a structure that was bigger than his, and it stood as firm.'

It was only years later that Raj learned that the choice for steel in the United States as the material for the first space frame had been as much a pragmatic choice as his in India was for concrete. He tells us: 'I learned that the first space frame was built from this steel just to prove that it could be done. At the time, there was a lot of shell material [for armaments] available in the States that hadn't been used. Those were war leftovers. It was as a matter of convenience and never a conscious choice to do the space frame in steel only.'

According to Raj, steel is still preferred today for space frames, despite the advantages of concrete, because it suits European countries and their building traditions. 'In addition, it suits the industry very well. It is very quick to do a space frame in steel.' For India, however, he is convinced that concrete still works better. 'In India we have a sufficient supply of labour, and generally these workers are not so well trained. Using concrete is easy: all they have to do is throw the concrete and fix the steel parts. That suits the Indian situation.'

THE NEXT GENERATION

After the Permanent Exhibition Complex, a long list of now iconic buildings followed: among others the Nehru Memorial Pavilion, the Asian Games Olympic Village, the Sheikh Sarai Group Housing, the National Institute of Immunology, the State Trading Corporation, the World Bank, and Parliament Library. These projects have in common not just that they are all located in Delhi, but also, interestingly, that they were all commissioned by government or semi-government clients. With his having done so many social and institutional projects during his career, we wonder what Raj's advice is for the new generation of Indian architects. Do they need to opt for either social or for commercial work? Or is it possible or even advisable to combine the two in one practice?

'I think we were a bit lucky, me, Charles Correa, our generation', Raj says, after thinking it over for some time. 'We could have made the choice between doing commercial and social architecture, but we did not have to make it. Nowadays, even if architects have the same mindset as I and my peers had, the scene they have to work in is different. There is simply not much institutional or housing work you can do for the state. You have to work with commercial parties.' And that will neither always be easy nor will it provide the best environment for young architects, Raj thinks. 'Because of the speed with which projects are developed and buildings constructed, the scene is currently very commercial and competitive. A major problem is that Indian promoters, though very good at making money, are architecturally illiterate.'

Nevertheless, Raj is optimistic about the future: 'I expect that in five to ten years there may be some architects that can persuade them [the commercial clients]. Although in the current scene and with current clients you have to work faster, for larger numbers, and in unfavourable situations, I am sure that good architects can meet all these requirements in due time and make great architecture.'

DELHI URBAN ART COMMISSION AND SLUMS

In 2011 Raj himself took up a new role and became the Chairman of the Delhi Urban Arts Commission (DUAC). After a few moments of doubt whether to take up the job–'I thought for an artist to join the establishment would be the kiss of death'–he decided that it would be worth it as it would 'possibly be the only way to make some serious studies about Delhi's housing problems'.

The Commission had been set up in the 1970s to advise the national and local government in Delhi on preserving and developing 'the aesthetic quality of urban and environmental design in Delhi'. Its mandate was thus to act as an advisory body regarding building proposals that could affect the skyline or the surroundings. However, as Chairman, Raj managed to change the entire outlook of the Commission.

'The Commission's normal work had nothing to do with housing of the poor', he explains. 'We were supposed to judge formal buildings. I said I'd find it a waste of time to tell another architect what he should and should not do. And I said that what we should do instead is to draft clear construction rules that any architect or builder in Delhi needs to follow; rules such as regarding the permanent finish and the quality of foundations for example. I told everyone that if architects would stick to the rules, there would be no need for them to come to us to get their plans approved.'

This streamlining freed the hands of the Commission to focus on the housing problems of the poor. Raj says: 'Delhi's slums may be comparatively nicer than those of Bombay, but that doesn't mean that having fifty per cent of your population living in unauthorized buildings isn't a huge problem. I joined the Urban Arts Commission as through it I hope to find solutions to improve the living conditions for Delhi's poor. First, I persuaded the Minister to give us some money to conduct studies. And next, I started creating a small office with a team of fifteen people, including urban designers, architects, and whoever else is motivated to uncover the problems and the solutions. Our common aim is to see if and how we can–with simple interventions–improve living conditions. We plan to publish our suggestions, bring them to the attention of the municipal corporation, and try to speak to the humanity of those in power.'

When we ask what has so far been the output of the DUAC, Raj says: 'One problem that stood out from the beginning is the absence of toilets and bathrooms. So we have done a study on how we can best develop public toilets. I designed these toilets myself.' He pauses for a moment and then adds chuckling: 'They could be my last project.'

PERMANENT EXHIBITION COMPLEX, PRAGATI MAIDAN, DELHI

PARLIAMENT LIBRARY BUILDING, DELHI

STATE TRADING CORPORATION (STC), DELHI

STC
टॉलस्टाय मार्ग
RFG-JV

QUTAB MINAR, DELHI

MY DELHI

RAJ REWAL

DELHI IS SPECIAL BECAUSE

I'm not so sure Delhi is special. It is special maybe because it is–and always in some way has been–the capital of the country? Maybe it is special because its history precedes the various colonial periods? In the context of the seven cities that were built, destroyed and rebuilt, maybe the city is a bit special.

THIS CAN BE IMPROVED

Many things, but one disadvantage that the city of Delhi really has is that it is very spread out. It does not have a nucleus at the moment. I would like to create that if I can. I would like to create a boulevard that links Rajpath with the Ramlila Ground. Historically, that is the open space of the city. It would be nice to connect the two. I wrote a paper about it some time back, but didn't follow it up. It requires tremendous political will to execute such a plan.

MY FAVOURITE PLACE

When we were children, we used to make weekend trips with our parents to the monuments in Delhi, such as Humayun's Tomb and the Qutab Minar. Getting there then was so different than it is now: Delhi had one-twentieth of the current population! What hasn't changed, however, are the gardens around the monuments. They are still nice, and we are lucky in Delhi to not have one or two such parks, but many.

THE BEST PLACE TO RELAX

My own home.

MY CHOICE OF TRANSPORTATION

When I was very young it used to be a cycle. Now that is too dangerous for me. I have a driver now. Although I do not cycle myself anymore, I do work on the 'cyclability' of Delhi. We have made improving the city for cyclists and pedestrians one of the aims set for the Urban Art Commission.

MY FAVOURITE LANDMARK

That would still be Humayun's Tomb. I lived right in front of it for twelve years. Its iconic form surrounded by a large garden is the basis of all Moghul monuments. Its internal space has been traced back by historians to Buddhist mandala structures which had a central sacred space around which you could move around. The Moghuls adopted the symmetrical form in their tombs and put the graveyard in the centre.

WHAT I LIKE ABOUT DELHI

Apart from student years in London and Paris, I have always lived in Delhi. It is a city where I have close connections. I don't know if I love the city; I think it has grown too fast. But when you live in a city for such a long time, you will always find some parts where you relate to. One thing Delhi has, compared to other cities, is lots of open spaces. I like that about Delhi. We have beautiful trees. Very few cities of the world have such wonderful trees. That's a nice part, and it makes that there is no need to escape the city.

WHAT WE CAN LEARN FROM DELHI

I can only give a very negative answer. We can learn a lot about things we should not be doing, or should have done, but haven't. Pollution is a problem. Our public transport should be better. Our gardens should be related to each other in a much nicer way. We should have pedestrianized parts of the city. All these things we haven't done.

Delhi is not a place where you learn something. It is a place where you can do something. It isn't finished yet. I do think that there is a scope for redesigning Delhi on its periphery and rehouse its slums and ever increasing population in a humane manner which can be properly connected by the new metro rail network.

TREES OF DELHI

PRADIP KRISHEN

Pradip Krishen (1949) studied History at Delhi and Oxford Universities and started his working life teaching history at a college in Delhi University. After a few years he realized he wanted to become a filmmaker. Between 1976 and 1979 he made a series of fifteen-minute science documentaries for India's national TV channel Doordarshan, and later, three feature films: *Massey Sahib, In Which Annie Gives It Those Ones*, and *Electric Moon*. His second film about architecture students at Delhi's School of Planning and Architecture, went on to become a cult classic.

In the mid-1990s, Krishen shifted his focus once again. He stopped making films and directed his attention to trees and plants. Over the past two decades, he has taken up a variety of roles. He worked as an advisor on a biodiversity park, organized nature walking tours, took up advocacy of endangered areas, and authored several books and brochures on trees and plants.

His present projects include the creation of a desert rock park with native plants around the Mehrangarh Fort in Jodhpur and most recently, the beginnings of a botanic trail with native montane plants in the north-western Himalaya. His latest book, *Jungle Trees of Central India*, was published by Penguin in 2014.

'I never thought I'd be professionally involved with trees or plants. I always loved being in wild places, but for the longest time I really didn't ask too many questions.' Environmentalist, activist, and landscape architect avant la lettre Pradip Krishen smiles when he makes the confession. He realizes that the walls of the study in his New Delhi home where we meet for our interview seem to tell another story, packed as they are from ground to ceiling with books on trees and ecology.

After three years of making short science documentaries for India's national TV channel Doordarshan, as well as feature films (among which is the cult classic *In Which Annie Gives It Those Ones*), Krishen felt his career as a filmmaker had arrived at a juncture where he had to choose to 'either go to Bombay and go commercial or find something new'. Around the same time, he became involved with a small town on the edge of the jungle in the state of Madhya Pradesh that was being threatened by unsustainable tourism. 'It triggered an interest for ecological planning. I realized this was the "something new" I had been looking for.'

He decided to give up filmmaking, and the next two years were spent working on the endangered township, collaborating with various groups, committees, and organizations. Meanwhile, he educated himself on everything related to the natural environment. The historian-turned filmmaker reinvented himself once again, this time as an environmental activist, conservationist, educator, and ecological landscaper; a multitude of hats he has donned ever since.

TREES OF DELHI ... AND ELSEWHERE

In 2006 Krishen published *Trees of Delhi-A Field Guide*. As the title suggests, the book catalogues and describes all the trees he could find in the city of Delhi. Explaining the genesis of his first book, Krishen says: 'I had spent some years struggling to do things in the planning sphere. It was quite clear that I had made very little headway. Now I wanted to take up something terribly simple, something I could do on my own and did not need to rely on others for. I set out to make a little booklet on the trees you can find in Delhi. My plan was to finish it in a year or so. However, along the way it became more and more ambitious. One year became two, and in the end it took me all of six years.'

The time spent on researching and writing *Trees of Delhi* turned out to be worthwhile: once published, it not only quickly became the standard work for anyone who wanted to know more about the plant life in the capital city, it also became a commercial success, with over 18,000 copies sold.

Working on *Trees of Delhi*, it struck Krishen again and again that most of the capital's trees are exotics and not very suitable for the city's arid land climate. They need large amounts of water, which is impossible and unsustainable in a city that suffers year upon year from water shortages. Almost without realizing it, he had found his new mission: to conserve existing landscapes of native plants, to create landscapes where native plants predominate, and to educate people on the value and beauty of India's indigenous plants.

MANGAR BANI

Krishen's work in and around the Manga Bani forest is a good example of his work to highlight existing landscapes. This forest is located on the border of New Delhi and Haryana, along the Gurgaon-Faridabad Highway. With Delhi's satellite city Gurgaon booming, and land prices skyrocketing, many villagers decided to cash in and sell their plots in the surrounding villages. Simultaneously, the pressure on the local government mounted to put the 100 hectares of communal forestland on the real estate market.

Says Krishen: 'For decades this beautiful forest was regarded as the communal land of the pastoral Gujjar community. The soil of this forest is unsuitable for farming and pasture. Not being able to use it for any other purpose, the villagers consecrated the forest in the memory of a baba, a holy man, who is believed to have vanished in a cave in the area. They believe that cutting even a branch of a tree in the forest will invite the baba's wrath. The result: a pristine area where many species spectacularly adapted to rocky areas still thrive. One of them–Dhau or Anogeissus pendula–is a habitat specialist. If Dhau trees are removed, nothing else will replace it. The area is too dry and too rocky for seeds to germinate on their own.'

Krishen holds no illusions that he can prevent the villagers from selling their land for the incredible sums developers have to offer. 'We can't stop the villagers', he argues, 'but what we can do, is raise awareness of the ecological importance of this forest and try to stop the government from making the community land into a commodity. It is such a beautiful and unique landscape, we simply can't afford to let it go without any resistance.'

THE RIDGE

Krishen's deep passion for Delhi's natural environment is also shown by his engagement with the Delhi Ridge, a forested hilly area that runs in a 35-kilometre-long arc along the west side of the capital. Krishen calls the Ridge 'his training ground'. It is divided in four zones, the Northern, Central, South-Central and Southern Ridge, and he tries to visit the zone that is closest to his home, the Central Ridge, almost every day. Apart from enjoying it on morning or evening walks in solitude or in the company of his five beagles, he also regularly takes people on what he calls tree walks to try and spread awareness about the Ridge and why it is important to the city.

It was during one of those tree walks, that Krishen shared with us the remarkable story of an intriguing former resident of the Ridge, a woman who claimed to be the Begum of Oudh, a former princely state which centred around the city of Lucknow. 'In the 1970s, a lady approached the government of India and claimed she was a descendant of the Nawab of Oudh', Krishen tells. 'In the 1850s this prince had been dethroned by the British and his properties were seized. Now, this lady wanted compensation on the grounds that she was the descendent of a family that had been one of India's first Freedom Fighters. The government, however, didn't take her claims seriously, and in any case was unsure of here antecedents. The lady had no papers to prove her lineage, but threatened to occupy the First Class waiting room of the New Delhi railway station if her demands were not met. And so it happened: not only did she move into the waiting room, she set up home there, accompanied by her two children, a troop of servants, about a dozen dogs, and even her chandeliers. She did not allow train passengers, or anyone else, to enter her new home.'

Initially, the government ignored her, but she turned out to be more stubborn than it had expected. 'She meant it when she said: "I am not going to move until you give me a place". She stayed in the waiting room for eight years! Finally, around 1984, the government decided to allot her a house: a dilapidated, ancient hunting lodge on the Ridge, called Bistdari [some people call it Malcha Mahal]. This is where she lived until, some people say, she committed suicide in royal style. She swallowed a mixture of poison and crushed diamonds. Her son and daughter still live in the lodge, but do not come out very often.'

Although we are eager to see the lodge after hearing the story, we have to curb our curiosity. Krishen says it can't be seen from the footpaths in the forest, nor can it be approached, as there is a fence around it. What he does show us are the rusty semi-overgrown gates to the home of the illustrious family. He brings to our attention the signboard attached to the gate. The gate and the signboard with its messy yet unambiguous text befit the fairy tale-like story, reading: Entry Restricted. Cautious of Hound Dogs. Proclamation. Intruders Shall Be Gundown.

AUTHORITIES

As we continue our walk through the Ridge, Krishen reveals that his dream project would be to work right there. Given the opportunity, he would like to remove all the exotic trees and plants, and reintroduce species that were once native to the Ridge. Yet, he knows that on his terms and conditions this is unlikely to happen. 'I would want a guarantee that the restoration work would have some sanctity. A guarantee that after I'm done no one else can meddle with it and create an ornamental garden or so. Especially not any civic or government bodies.'

Seeing the question marks on our faces, Krishen elaborates. He admits that so far the government's involvement with the Ridge has been minimal, but he emphasizes that 'wherever it has intervened, the outcome has always been disappointing.' 'Take for example the Budhha Jayanti Park that the Central Public Works Department (CPWD) carved out of the Ridge. The CPWD has no understanding of the kind of ecology they were planting in, no sensitivity at all to the landscape. They simply tried to create another Lodhi Garden with the same suite of plants inside the rocky, thin-soiled Ridge. So then they had a whole lot of thirsty plants that needed constant watering to survive. And were forced to lay huge water pipelines to make their survival possible! Yet not for one second did they reflect on how ridiculous all this was.'

'Or take the engagement of the responsible authority–the Forest Department–with the Ridge', he continues. 'You hardly ever see them except for a few days at the end of each financial year. Then suddenly armies of labourers come to plant jamun trees. The jamun is a riverside tree. It cannot survive in dry conditions on the Ridge. But do you think the Forest Department cares? No, all they care about is that they should spend all the money allocated to them, so that at least their budget for the next year is safe'. Krishen pauses to take a breath and concludes: 'You can see why I would much rather have the government stay away from the Ridge.'

MEHRANGARH FORT

'One of the main challenges in taking up new green projects is to find someone who owns land and has the same commitment to the project', Krishen found. 'A building is not so easy to destroy', he explains. 'But destroying a garden in one day or week is possible. That's why it is so important to choose your clients and projects carefully.'

A project he accepted after due consideration was the restoration of a large tract of volcanic rock land adjoining the 15th century Mehrangarh Fort, in Jodhpur, Rajasthan. Originally built in the fifth century, this mud fort was rebuilt several times in subsequent centuries. About a decade ago it attracted attention once anew, and restoration work began.

'The initial request to me was to "green the area"', Krishen remembers. 'I think what they meant was, if I could design a garden, and plant some trees as a way of creating an attractive adjunct space in the immediate environs of the Fort. That is probably what any standard landscape architect in India would have done ... Bring in palm trees and flowering ornamentals with lots of elaborate irrigation. I told the Trust which controls the Fort that the only sensible way of proceeding would be to attempt to restore the ecology of this rocky tract, to try and bring back all the plants that are superbly adapted to live and survive in desert rock in this part of the world. It took them a few weeks to evaluate what this would involve, but to its credit, the Trust responded by saying, "When can you start?" That was how we began creating the Rao Jodha Desert Rock Park in 2006.

The project not only resulted in a beautiful park, it also taught Krishen and his team a lot about desert ecology and how plants manage to colonize inhospitable rocky terrain. For example, Krishen found that one of the crucial plant associations that result in the colonization of rock (by plants) is a short grass called Oropetium and an associated liverwort. Together, these form 'starter mats' on rock which make it possible for other small plants, forbs and grasses, to grow on horizontal surfaces. In his work, Krishen began to use these 'starter mats' as a way of accelerating the growth of native plants on the rocky terrain.'

THE FUTURE

At the time of our interview Krishen was busy producing several booklets for the information centre of the Rao Jodha Park. These booklets cover various species of flora and fauna in the park and are wonderfully designed. Krishen himself took most of the beautiful photographs.

Photography is something he learned working on his latest book, *The Jungle Trees of Central India*, the other writing project that kept him busy over the past years. 'To make this book I needed to undertake almost forty field trips', Krishen says. 'I would wake up early, travel for an hour, walk for another hour, and arrive in time for the right light. It would have been impossible to get a photographer to invest the same amount of time as I did, so I took up the job myself.' Published by Penguin Books in 2014, *The Jungle Trees of Central India* describes the natural wild trees in an area the size of France.

It is not a coincidence that all his written work is, as Krishen himself calls it, "fieldguidey". 'The technical books that already exist are really dry scientific books that can only be understood by other botanists. I wanted to create simple, accessible, and engaging books. I want my readers to say: "We can enjoy learning about the trees we see around us without feeling frightened by scientific terms."'

With his latest writing project nearing completion, Krishen is already thinking about his next project. 'Maybe I'll do a small book on the desert. Or on the new sandy salty shrubland we discovered south of Jaisalmer and that has not yet been described. Or maybe I do one on the amazing variety of grasses in the desert, my latest love.' Krishen says it all with a look on his face as if he can't wait to start writing. Going by his earlier works, we can only hope he does.

PLANTING IN GULLY WALLS - GARDENERS PLACING PLANTS IN A ROCKY WALL (JODHPUR, RAJASTHAN)

DEVKUND: A SMALL LAKE AT ONE CORNER OF THE PARK THAT WAS PROBABLY CREATED ABOUT 200 YEARS AGO BY BUILDING A CAUSEWAY

ALONG ONE EDGE, DEVKUND IS VISITED BY A SURPRISINGLY LARGE NUMBER OF MIGRANT BIRDS IN WINTER (JODHPUR, RAJASTHAN)

VC & GARDEN POST-RAIN - RAO JODHA PARK'S VISITORS CENTRE IS HOUSED IN A 16TH CENTURY 'POL'. THE POL HAD FALLEN INTO DISUSE AND ITS ENTRANCE

WAS BRICKED UP, BUT IT NOW WELCOMES VISITORS INTO A SMALL ROCKY GARDEN THAT HAS BECOME A HAVEN FOR BUTTERFLIES (JODHPUR, RAJASTHAN)

ENTRY TO RED TRAIL - THE PARK HAS 4 MAJOR (AND MANY MINOR) WALKING TRAILS WHICH TAKE VISITORS THROUGH DIFFERENT KINDS OF

ROCKY DESERT HABITAT (JODHPUR, RAJASTHAN)

DELHI RIDGE

PRADIP KRISHEN

DELHI IS SPECIAL BECAUSE

Delhi is a special city for me because I have lived here almost my whole life. I watched it grow and change. There are parts of it that I still like very much, but there also large areas and developments that make me sad. I don't think I could say that I love Delhi as a physical space. But it has a great intellectual life, and plenty interesting people

THIS CAN BE IMPROVED

Traffic in the city is a huge problem. There are simply too many cars. We are pouring 10,000 cars onto our roads each month. That's frightening.

MY FAVOURITE PLACE

The central Ridge. The best time of the day to visit it is the early evening, just before sunset. I have no favourite season. I like it through all the different seasons. In September, at the end of the monsoon, the forest is lush green. Paths that are normally clear are overgrown, and need to be cleared again. Winter is the 'busiest' season in the forest: I see lots of people who come to collect firewood. Not all paths may have been cleared by the time summer arrives, but because it is so dry, it gets easier and easier to navigate through the trees and shrubs as the seasons progress.

THE BEST PLACE TO RELAX

For many people here it would be a club or a cultural institution. But for me it would be the Ridge. I am not a member of any club. Instead, I like walking. I relax by walking in the forest with my dogs or alone.

MY FAVOURITE RESTAURANT

Delhi has become much more interesting as a foodie place; there's more and more choice. I'm not sure if I have a favourite. If I was looking to go and have a Mughlai-style meal, I'd probably go to Havemore Restaurant in Pandara Market. It used to be a little dhaba-style place, but it has now gone upmarket. The food is still very good, though.

MY FAVOURITE LANDMARK

The Qutab Minar and its grounds, for two reasons. It has some very unusual trees, some of which I suspect are quite old. And it has got some slightly wild, unkempt parts I really like.

READY FOR DEMOLITION

Some of the government structures and offices that were built in the 1960s. I can't think of any particular building that I dislike most. There are many!

MY FAVOURITE DELHI MOVIE

Frankly, I don't know of any movies on Delhi, apart from my own. [Krishen refers to cult classic *In Which Annie Gives It Those Ones*].

MY FAVOURITE DELHI BOOK

I really enjoyed a book written by Upinder Singh, the daughter of former Prime Minister Manmohan Singh. It is entitled *Ancient Delhi*. Unlike most books in the genre it is a very readable account of what we know about the ancient history of Delhi. I enjoyed that!

WHAT WE CAN LEARN FROM DELHI

In many ways, Delhi is an eloquent lesson in how not to plan. Delhi has completely messed up all the advantages it once had. It has done a terrible job of planning specially in the last decades. There was ample opportunity around the time of Independence. We have turned our backs on the river and allowed it to become a sewer. We ignore the Ridge–and it's a miracle it still survives. And it's a terribly cruel city for the urban poor. I think part of the answer lies in decentralization. We should be desperately planning for other cities.

DEVELOPING MODERN INDIA

MOHIT GUJRAL

Mohit Gujral (1959) studied Architecture at CEPT University Ahmedabad. Subsequently, he became the Principal Architect and Chief Designer at Design-plus Architecture and set up Delanco Real Estate, a real estate company in association with DLF (Delhi Land and Finance). Well known buildings include the Great Eastern Centre on Nehru Place in Delhi, South Delhi luxury malls Promenade and Emporio, DLF Cyber Greens Technology Park in Gurgaon. In 2008 Gujral joined DLF Limited as Vice Chairman and Managing Director of one of the developing verticals. In 2014 he became Whole-time Director and Member of Corporate Social Responsibility Committee of DLF Limited and Chairman of DLF Universal Limited, a subsidiary company. He is also on the Board of several other companies.

The office is what one would expect of the office of the Whole-time Director of India's largest real estate developing company. It covers nearly the entire ninth floor of a Triple A location overlooking the heart of Delhi. A sizable portion of the office is decorated with comfortable Chesterfield chairs and sofas. The walls are filled with an art collection that any museum would be proud to exhibit. A TV visible from all corners of the room spew the latest 'breaking news' at a low volume. Apart from a few framed family pictures, the massive teak desk in the middle of the room is bare. Behind it sits Mohit Gujral. He keeps one eye on the TV while we discuss his past as an architect, his present as a developer, and his future as both.

ARCHITECT AT DESIGN PLUS

Mohit Gujral started his career at Design Plus (DP), the architecture firm established by his legendary father, Satish Gujral. Not an architect by training, but a painter and sculptor, father Gujral had an organic design style that emphasized the use of bricks, domes, and courtyards. His masterpiece is no doubt the Belgian Embassy in New Delhi. 'The time of the Belgian Embassy was the time that I joined the firm', Gujral shares. 'My father got ill when he was working on it. I dropped out of college to come and help him. I helped make a lot of changes in the design. At the time I was very much influenced by the Italian architect Carlo Scarpa, so I brought in Scarpa elements, into the external and interior details. I loved the scale of Scarpa's works, the way he articulated materials. He knew how to make a building far more alive than it actually is. For me this building was really my christening, my incubation in the world of architecture.'

COMMERCIAL GIANT

Despite his admiration for the Italian architect and his own father, Gujral moved the firm into another direction soon after he took over the reign. The designs started to reveal a preference for the use of modern materials, such as steel, glass, and granite. With this new approach, projects of a wide variety followed, including office buildings, retail outlets, and hospitality interiors. It was the BPO (Business Process Outsourcing) and telecom revolution that gave Design Plus its big break. Large shopping malls for DLF, corporate headquarters for a plethora of companies, private hospitals, hotels, and various townships followed a series of back offices for international companies. By the early 2000s, Gujral had transformed the office from a 'very niche boutique firm' into a commercial giant. At its peak Design Plus held an annual portfolio of 20 million square feet, with projects totalling about INR 20 billion.

THE MERGER

In 2008, real estate and infrastructure giant DLF asked Gujral to join the firm as Vice Chairman and Managing Director of one of its development verticals. Gujral accepted the offer and with it Design Plus (and Delanco, Gujral's real estate venture) merged with DLF. The step came as a surprise to many, Gujral recalls. 'In India it is not common for people to make such a big change when things are going well. People couldn't believe that I walked away from what I was doing [at Design Plus].' Although for Gujral life changed quite a bit, for the company much remained the same. Over the years DP had become one of DLF's principal architects, a position shared with Mumbai's Hafeez Contractor. 'At the time of the merge Design Plus had 40% of its business with DLF.'

Interestingly, despite the now more than close ties, DLF is not mentioned a single time on the website of Design Plus. When we ask why, Gujral says that it is because there is 'no involvement of DLF other than being an equity partner'. 'DLF wanted me', he says matter-of-factly. 'So they had to buy the equity to avoid conflict of interest of my time. They became partners in Design Plus by default. It's that simple.'

BUILDINGS OF CONSEQUENCE

'Large developers are often blamed for copy-pasting unimaginative designs and for avoiding the responsibility to create more interesting skylines.' Having experience in the world of construction in India both as an architect and as a developer, we wonder which of these two Gujral thinks has the ultimate power to set architecture agendas. with the developers. But he qualifies his statement instantly: 'What is important to remember is that immediate business, economic, and policy contexts matter a great deal in what developers can and what they want to do.'

The business context is simple. 'As a developer I am going to sell only what people want, and for now that is large glass buildings', says Gujral. 'It will take more time before clients stop following the West blindly only because they believe "West is Best". It will take more time before they ask themselves instead "What is really India?" "What is our own identity?" Here and there you see people who realize that all these glass buildings–well–are rather hot in this climate and not the best solution for us [in India]. People who work in those buildings start saying "I wish we had done a more ecofriendly building". But for now it is still mostly what people want. And as a developer that is what I will sell.'

With regard to the policy context Gujral points out how 'doing philanthropy in the West is very interesting, because it is tax-free'. This set-up, he argues, has made available large endowments and funds for great public works, museums, and the arts, and, as a result, has yielded great architecture. India's policies on the other hand, 'haven't evolved to that level yet'.

Finally, the current phase of economic development and the slowdown in economic growth are further to blame, says Gujral. 'We are in the middle of a building revolution, but still stuck at the stage where we are creating back office buildings for multinationals. That is also why you see a lot of these glass structures around. The work being done in these buildings has no doubt brought jobs and new aspirations. But the real wealth still has to be created. Only when that happens will we be able to start building buildings of consequence.' Gujral thinks this stage is merely 'a good five years away'. 'As soon as the economy starts picking up, we will witness a real architecture renaissance in India', he prophesizes. Yet, despite the power he holds, the renaissance won't start in his office. Indeed, the demand for it will have to come from the client first.

DLF'S DEBT

There are clear signs that DLF, like most other companies working in the field of construction, has been affected by the economic slowdown. The company is no longer buying land, and has sold off all the land it held in Mumbai. They are building at a much slower pace than before, and are in the papers not only for an INR 630 crore (one crore is 10 million) fine slammed on by the Competition Commission of India, but also for its mind-boggling debt of USD 5 billion.

Still, Gujral is optimistic. Is it because he realizes DLF is almost, to use that catchy phrase of the economic crisis, 'too big to fail'? He doesn't tell us so in so many words. Instead he says: 'If you survive this time, that will be wonderful. Many won't be able to survive. DLF can hold on because the banks still believe in the company based on our assets and income. Our assets are multiples of our debt. Plus we get a very, very large income from our rentals. We don't have a debt servicing problem.'

Unlike large developers in the West, DLF follows a model of holding on to assets. 'We have sold all our residential real estate, but most of the retail and office buildings we built are still owned by us. We continue to build. That is one of the reasons why our debt is so high. The other is the way borrowing funds works here. Whereas all around the world you borrow at a lower rate than you rent, in India that is the other way around. We borrow at 14 percent and rent at 8 ... That means there is always a negative cash flow of 6 percent.' Seeing our puzzled faces, he pauses for a second and adds: 'The question simply becomes how long can you hold on.' And DLF, because of its sheer size, can hold on–most likely an entire economic crisis long.

RESIDENTIAL & RETAIL

Despite the debts and the economic slowdown, Gujral is not worried that India will wake up to find the real estate market as much of a bubble as it turned out to be in some parts of the world. 'India is different', he explains. 'One of the ways in which it is different is that unlike buyers in the West, Indians are extremely conservative when it comes to buying a home. People don't borrow what they can't afford, if they borrow at all. When people read in the newspapers the economy is going down, you see immediately that they stop buying homes. They will only buy when they are sure they have a job tomorrow and know they can service their own home. This makes that the leverage is extremely backed and secure. What happened in the West is that the leverage got sold 100 times over. Nobody cared to check the credit of the customer. It was a financial game played by the banks, the investment banks. In India, this didn't happen because people don't borrow what they can't afford and because the Reserve Bank is extremely strong on compliance and risk. So therefore the risk, in a real estate world from a customer perspective, is not more than

10–20%. The real estate market on long term is very healthy story for India.'

The economic slowdown did cause changes in the market and in the DLF portfolio. They have more or less stopped building commercial structures and shifted their focus on residential and retail complexes. They concentrate on both because there is still a strong demand and because these are safe markets. 'Retail is the lowest common factor to spend money', Gujral explains the continuing success of retail. 'Going to the mall, buying clothes, living out your aspirations, these are accessible to all.' Even though retail is doing very well in India, the character and thus the design and set-up of malls are changing. The success of online shopping is the cause. Says Gujral: 'With online shopping now having become an important sales channel malls are less and less places where goods are traded, and more and more showrooms, and leisure and hospitality destinations.'

TODAY'S AND TOMORROW'S PROJECTS

Currently Gujral works mostly on upgrading the infrastructure of Gurgaon, where DLF owns most of its land. The company says it is investing USD 150 million to make Gurgaon into an urban park. 'The urban planning was very haphazard in that area', Gujral explains the project. 'We didn't own all the land in one go. The land policy of the time didn't allow you to do so. That has changed now and we can own large plots. In retrospect we are now constructing bridges and tunnels to make the entire Gurgaon into an urban park. We will integrate the whole experience of living and working in the city.' And, needless to say, increase the value of their land and buildings by doing so.

When we ask him about his dream project, something he wants to do in the future, we find that Gujral does not dream the dreams of an architect, but truly those of a smart and creative entrepreneur: 'My dream? To build India's first ski resort where the complete winter sports lifestyle is offered. I got in at rough and difficult times (at DLF) and I hope that when the renaissance comes that I can profit from that, and build some great stuff.'

AMBIENCE ISLAND, GURGAON

Canon
RAPID METRO

AMBIENCE ISLAND, GURGAON

DLF

GURGAON METRO

TEE
CHD

AMBIENCE ISLAND, GURGAON

Experience Independence
DLF
WNS

LODHI GARDENS, DELHI

DELHI IS SPECIAL BECAUSE

It is a very diverse city: in topography, in historical influences, in the number and type of green areas, in people. Delhi is the political capital, but also the cultural capital of India. It is a dynamic place, where people with the influence to create change come together. That makes it an interesting city to be. But if you ask me on a very personal level why this city is special to me, the answer would simply be 'because I have lived here almost all my life'. I think that even if the place where you live is 'junk', you will still develop an emotive connect if you spend enough time there.

THIS CAN BE IMPROVED

Two things: infrastructure and public art. We still have a long way to go in terms of infrastructure. That has simply to do with the sheer size of the city. Indian cities are not designed to walk in. This will change if we redensify our cities.

We also need to have more public art. I come from an artistic family and I know there is a lot of good art in India. Unfortunately you will find it only inside buildings. At present one cannot donate anything to be placed in parks or public spaces. For example, if I want to donate a sculpture made by my father to the city of Delhi it is impossible to do so, because there are no guidelines and policies for it. I hope this will change in the near future. My wife is currently working on drafting a bill on cultural social responsibility. The aim of this bill is precisely to allow corporates to donate art to public spaces.

MY FAVOURITE PLACE

Being an architect, I enjoy walking in Lodhi Garden, right next to my house. I love walking through the nature, the historical buildings. It is very refreshing and enriching. It is my daily recharge for the senses.

THE BEST PLACE TO RELAX

My home and the golf club.

MY FAVOURITE RESTAURANT

I quite like the restaurant in hotel The Lodhi, but part of that is pure convenience: I only like to go five minutes away from my house. Khan Market is also buzzing and very economical.

MY FAVOURITE LANDMARK

Humayun's Tomb. It is far less hyped than the Taj Mahal and very accessible. I like the scale of it, the details. It doesn't have that stark white of the Taj. Instead, the way marble and stone are morphed is wonderful and very emotive. I shouldn't overanalyse it. It's simply a beautiful building and a great park to walk. It's just that.

READY FOR DEMOLITION

Cleaning up can rejuvenate large parts of Delhi. That type of urban intervention is the change that Delhi needs. I would not demolish anything. The ugliness is also part of what Delhi is. That's what we are. There is no point in trying to change Delhi. If you want everything perfect, you better move to New Jersey or so.

MY FAVOURITE BUILDING

The Belgian Embassy. My father built it, and it is where I started my own career as an architect. The outside doesn't reveal the best parts. You have to go inside to really see it. Father got knighted for that building.

WHAT WE CAN LEARN FROM DELHI

Delhi, like all cities, is dynamic and changing constantly. Every visit you will find it different: in terms of economics and even the people. We are now very close to the point that cities will compete to attract talent. How well they fare, has to do with what they have to offer. Delhi has a lot to offer, particularly in the Indian context. It has a rich history that is very visible, and despite all the congestion there is still a fair amount of green cover. We have a river, which, despite all its possibilities, we haven't even addressed yet. Being located right between Delhi and Noida, it is bound to be developed soon.

FROM THE NETHERLANDS TO INDIA … AND BEYOND

JOERI AULMAN

Joeri Aulman (1978) is an architect by training, with a Master of Science degree from Delft University of Technology in the Netherlands. Upon graduation he joined his current employer, Royal HaskoningDHV, as project manager, but after two years he left the firm to join the urban design and landscape architecture firm ACLA in Mumbai. Mumbai was a second home, since his wife hails from this city.

For ACLA, Aulman worked on a number of residential condominium projects, Special Economic Zone (SEZ) developments, and a plan for new recreational facilities at the Mumbai Racecourse. By sheer coincidence, NACO (Netherlands Airport Consultants), a company owned by his former employer Royal HaskoningDHV, landed a project in Mumbai in 2007, three years after he had moved there. Aulman did not hesitate and joined his former employer's subsidiary to work on the development of Mumbai Airport. Currently he lives in Mumbai, dividing his time between projects in Mumbai and Delhi.

An architect by training, over the past decade Joeri Aulman not only became an aviation infrastructure expert by profession, but something of an intercultural communication expert as well. Since 2005, the Dutchman has been working at Royal HaskoningDHV (RHDHV), which offers services in a wide variety of (engineering related) fields, one of them being airport planning, design, engineering, and development. Under the brand name Netherlands Airport Consultants (NACO), RHDHV engineers have worked on more than 550 airports worldwide. Aulman himself worked extensively in Mumbai, where he offered planning and design services to the new private owner of the airport. When it became clear that in order to do sustainable business in India the company would need to land another key client, he turned his attention to Delhi as well, and did so successfully. The past three years Aulman's focus has mainly been on Delhi Airport where he acquired three different projects for the company. At present, he divides his working hours between Delhi and Mumbai, as his company has been appointed to perform an Air Traffic Forecast for Mumbai Airport.

BRIDGE

'NACO works with a small aviation team in India, with close ties to a team of experts in the Netherlands', Aulman says. 'This is the best way to work in a field that depends very much on investment cycles. There are periods where we require lots of people on airport projects, followed by lean periods with less work. During peak periods the small team in India can rely on the general engineering capacity of the company, and in lean periods these engineers work on other infrastructure projects.'

Aulman is the bridge between the local Indian engineering team and staff based in the Netherlands. He also liaises with clients. In both guises solving communication gaps and managing expectations is an important aspect of his job. 'On a daily basis I am really bridging a cultural divide between two very different countries and cultures', he says. 'For instance, Indian clients strongly believe that something suggested by foreign experts that works abroad may not necessarily work in India. Thus, even our best ideas conveyed by our most senior experts are sometimes met with reluctance. However, if I convey these ideas to our clients, clients are more readily willing to accept them, since they feel I know the Indian context well enough to judge if the concept could work here. In this way, I have often been able to successfully introduce our global expertise locally.'

100 AIRPORTS

Whoever wonders if developing airports is not very much a niche sector, may not have realized how large India really is. 'There is certainly enough work to be done', says Aulman. 'More than enough, I'd almost say, as the Indian government has recently identified the need for an additional one hundred new airports in the country!' Seeing our surprise he adds: 'This need is based on both the appetite of the growing middle class for travel by air, for leisure and business, as well as a desire to connect remote parts of this enormous country. Many corners have thus far insufficiently been made accessible by traditional infrastructure, such as roads and railways.'

Even though the aim of the government is to have private parties build and manage these new airports, the government is a factor in each project. 'Every one of these new airports needs upfront investment in basic facilities to allow safe flight services', Aulman explains. 'Yet traffic will be low in the first few years. That is why private developers are not very interested in these projects, unless the government "sweetens the deal". The exact location of the first of these one hundred airports ultimately depends on how badly the government wants a new airport in a particular area and how much subsidy it is therefore willing to pay. In the rare occasion that a locations harbours real-estate interests for local developers, they may be willing to invest in the airport regardless of government subsidy, but this won't happen very often, given the remote nature of most of the proposed locations.'

PRIVATE CLIENTS

Aulman is no longer a stranger to the private sector. For a few years now his company's focus in the aviation sector in India has been to work for private clients. 'The Indian government decided to privatize even the airports in what they call the "metro cities" here, the mega-cities, such as Mumbai and Delhi. These airports have guaranteed traffic and make a good business case for developers. Privatization allowed developers to maximize their return at these airports. The government, in turn, profited from receiving a fixed revenue share from the developer; income they intend to use toward subsidizing the development of airports in remote regions.'

Aulman points out that, interestingly, the private developers that took control of the Mumbai and Delhi airports are both family-run development firms, otherwise a rarity in the global airport development world. 'An advantage of working with family businesses is that the top management can take quick decisions, in contrast to many bureaucratic government airport clients. But there is a disadvantage too. Decision-making can be whimsical at times, based on the intuitions of the individual family members.'

Importantly though, he feels that 'by and large these Indian private developers have understood the business of airports'. He illustrates this by pointing out that they have been quick to adopt the latest wisdom from profitable airports such as Amsterdam Airport Schiphol. 'Key to the profitability of such airports have been the strategies to augment the income from airside operations with non-aeronautical revenues. NACO was involved in the development of Schiphol's Airport City and Duty Free Retail and was able to share this experience with several Indian clients for new airports, such as the DMIC Alwar Aerotropolis, and for improvement of existing airports, such as Delhi and Mumbai.'

Ultimately, gaining trust is the key to success in this field, Aulman has found. 'Gaining the trust of the decision-makers in these private companies takes time. You need at least a couple of interactions with them. But once you have their trust, once they are convinced your company has the technical know-how and capacity to deliver projects in India, you will find your company on their shortlist. When the bidding process starts there will only be a select group of competitors. The final selection of who gets the job is based on technical evaluation and price. They generally are deemed equally important by the client.'

DELHI

In Delhi the gradual process of gaining trust resulted in winning a small project at first, followed in 2013 by a large assignment. 'Apart from making it to the shortlist, your company also needs to be able to offer a competitive fee. The only reason we were able to work against such competitive rates was because Royal HaskoningDHV's local general engineering resources were mobilized to deliver a large part of the project locally.'

The big project is the development and building of, what they call, a Cross Taxiway Bridge. Showing us images of the project Aulman says: 'The Cross Taxiway Bridge connects Delhi Airport's southern runway and taxiway system to its northern counterpart. It will improve the efficiency of aircraft ground movements: saving time, fuel, and emissions. The connection needs to be elevated, because it crosses the main airport access road. This makes it unique in India. Since NACO had completed the design of similar taxiway bridges at Schiphol and Frankfurt airport and we had the local general engineering support in India from our group company Royal HaskoningDHV, the owners of Delhi airport felt confident we could deliver the first such project in India.'

HICCUPS

But what is it really like, working in airport development in India? Were there any hiccups working in Delhi? Where did he encounter bottlenecks?

Aulman doesn't have to think long before sharing his experiences. 'A typical Delhi trait is the disregard for good finishes', he starts. 'Unfortunately, examples of this can be found literally at every corner in the city. We managed to break this trend at the airport, though. The higher regard at airports for the integrity of essential infrastructure and public facilities are to credit here; safety and public relations considerations prevalent at airports help a lot. But to assure the quality of the final product, we also have our own strategies. We have our tender documents specify the materials to be used in great detail. Only after we have checked that there is ample availability of these exact materials in Delhi, and after we have tested them, do we include them in the document. This way we prevent that contractors cite unavailability of certain materials in order to either inflate their costs or use inferior materials.'

In the case of Delhi the already existing relationship of trust made for a 'reasonably smooth project with only a few minor challenges'. These challenges, Aulman says, were overcome in close coordination with the client. 'The client wanted to have our technical expert present on a continuous basis in Delhi, for instance. Slowly we were able to bring this down to an "as and when required" basis. Further, a three-month delay in surveying activity due to heavy fogs did not result in major cost-overruns; this because our client was willing to allow the consultant to demobilize for that period. We felt that was a decision which proved the client's professionalism! And lastly, and most importantly, getting security clearance is a known bottleneck in airport projects. In our case we, the consultant and the client, jointly convinced the security authorities to provide the necessary approvals. I think that saved us a lot of time and energy'

'We were grateful for the flexibility displayed by the client in this project', Aulman says, 'and in recognition of our special relationship, we undertook some extra studies for them to help Delhi Airport become less prone to flooding during the monsoon rainy season, now and in the future.'

SKETCH AIRPORT PRIVATE JET TERMINAL, Indira Gandhi International Airport, Delhi

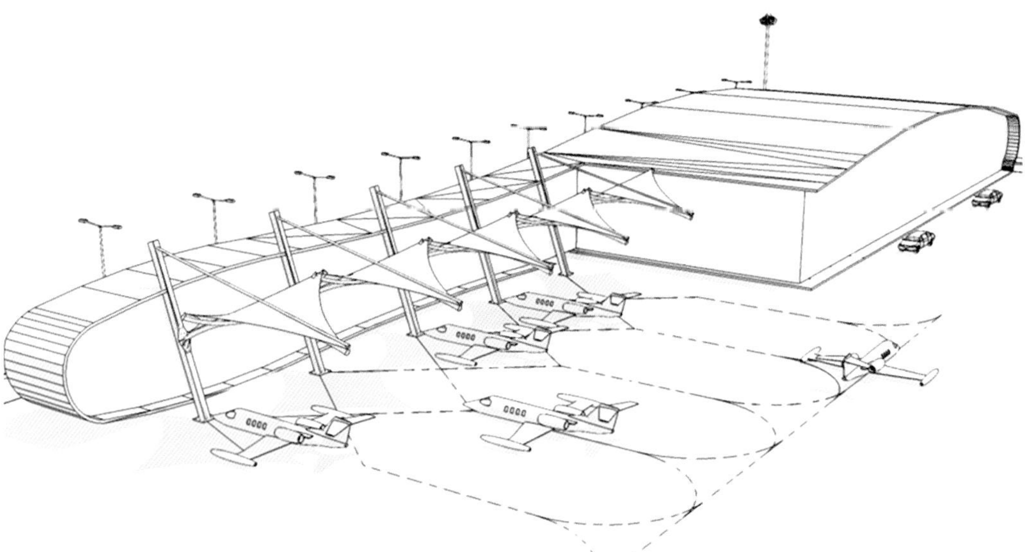

INTER STATE BUS TERMINUS, KASHMERE GATE, DELHI

MY DELHI

JOERI AULMAN

DELHI IS SPECIAL BECAUSE

Of its rich history. Over a period of nearly two thousand years, no less than seven consecutive cities were developed in the area we now call Delhi. Remains of these great cities can still be found all over the metropolitan landscape. That makes it a fascinating city to explore.

THIS CAN BE IMPROVED

Traffic! 'Fascinating' turns to 'horrendous' if you plan to explore the city during peak hours. I think the solution lies in multi-use, high-density development linked to the Metro system. That way, more people can live and work near high-quality public transport which will halt the proliferation of private vehicles in the city.

MY FAVOURITE PLACE

Lodhi Gardens. One of the seven cities built on the soil of Delhi was that of the Lodhis. The Lodhis were the last sultans of Delhi. Five hundred years later, their magnificent tombs were used as follies in the park of yet another city plan, that of Lutyens New Delhi. The resulting Lodhi Gardens are a magnificent example of the English Garden Style applied to a foreign setting, and they are a lovely place to wander around.

MY CHOICE OF TRANSPORTATION

If it has to be surface transport, I prefer an Ambassador taxi with air-conditioning. But preferably I don't move between locations too much, because a daunting aspect of working on a project in Delhi is the fact that traveling from, for instance, the company guesthouse to the office or to the client can take up to two hours one way! The traffic is chaotic and ever-increasing. For this reason I developed a pattern of flying into Delhi Airport from Mumbai, spending the full day in the client's airport office, and then making my way to the company guesthouse only in the late evening to avoid traffic. The next morning I would leave early for our office and convince the client to keep any further meetings till the next day, so I could go straight to the client's airport office early next morning, spend the whole day there and hop on a flight back to Mumbai in the evening.

MY FAVOURITE LANDMARK

Humayun's Tomb. Have you ever observed it from one of the bridges over Yamuna River? It is a truly remarkable sight from there!

MY FAVOURITE DELHI BOOK

The Last Mughal about the final days of the Mughal Empire which eclipsed in Delhi in 1854. It was written by William Dalrymple. The book gives great insight into the original nature of the city; a capital of culture. Even when the Mughal Empire had been reduced to a mere puppet of the British East India Company by the middle of the 19th century, it was still the epicentre of the Arts, due to the Mughal ruling elite's patronage of poets, painters, architects, sculptors, and craftsmen. Reading this fascinating book gave me great understanding of the painful schizophrenia the city has suffered ever since.

MY FAVOURITE DELHI FILM

Monsoon Wedding, *Delhi Belly* and *Delhi 6*. These movies expose the intrinsic cultural heterogenic nature of Delhi and its inherent skirmishes in a light and amusing way.

WHAT WE CAN LEARN FROM DELHI

Patience ... with the traffic, with the bureaucracy, patience with the low work ethic (no-no, not everyone!), but also valuable patience instilled by the sounds of the sitar on one of those cool Delhi evenings amongst its many magical historic locations making me realize that we need to calm down and reflect, that I believe will give Delhiites a strong sense of belonging and the strength to 'survive' the city. Without that, I feel many people would feel lost. It would be a shame if that sense of community disappears when everybody starts living in anonymous high-rise towers.

WORLD BANK INDIA

ONNO RUHL AND BARJOR MEHTA

Onno Ruhl (1961) is currently the World Bank Country Director for India. Prior to this assignment, he was the Director for Operations Services and Quality in the South Asia Region of the World Bank, and was responsible for the Quality Assurance, Development Effectiveness as well as core fiduciary functions for the South Asia portfolio of the World Bank. Before that, he worked in various African countries for the World Bank, and in various positions covering African, Central Asian and European regions.

Before joining the World Bank's staff, he worked at the Royal Netherlands Embassy in Washington DC as Economic Secretary, and was Alternate Director on the Board of the Multilateral Investment Guarantee Agency and Desk Officer in the Multilateral Development Cooperation Department of the Netherlands Ministry of Foreign Affairs. He started his career teaching economics in Alkmaar, the Netherlands.

Barjor Mehta (1958) is the Lead Urban Specialist in the World Bank's Global Practice on Social, Urban, Rural and Resilience, based in New Delhi, India. He moved to India in 2012 from the Bank's Dar es Salaam, Tanzania Country Office from where he worked on urban sector projects and programs in Tanzania, Uganda, Kenya, Sudan and South Sudan. Prior to that he was based in Washington DC from where he worked on Sierra Leone, Ethiopia, South Africa, Yemen, Iran, India, Sri Lanka and Pakistan. Before joining the Bank he was the Director, School of Planning, CEPT University, Ahmedabad. He has also lived and worked in Sri Lanka, Thailand and Bhutan. Barjor is an architect (CEPT, India) and urban planner (AIT, Thailand).

The World Bank's India portfolio consists of about USD 24 billion in investments in the country. The World Bank is involved in a wide range of projects: education, agriculture, roads, energy, health, cleaning up the river Ganges, sewage systems, and transportation projects. The India office is the second largest World Bank office in the world.

Delhi hosts its headquarters in two big offices. One office, designed by architect Raj Rewal, is located on Lodhi Road, while the other is in the former printing hall of the Hindustan Times on Connaught Place. One is, in the words of Country Director Onno Ruhl, 'a bit sleepy and old-fashioned', and the other 'more alive and urban'. Two sizable offices, but that is where the Bank's official engagement with Delhi ends. It has no projects in Delhi.

There are two reasons for this lack of involvement with the city, Onno Ruhl tells us. The first has to do with past mistakes made by the Bank, the second with the Bank's vision and strategy for the future. 'When Delhi proposed to build a metro system, we felt the city wasn't ready for it, did not need it, and that it would never be a success. Well, that was a mistake. We were very wrong! Luckily, the Japanese stepped in to do what we should have done. You can imagine it is not good for your organization's reputation to make such a misjudgement!' Ruhl continues: 'But even if we were more popular, we would not plan to engage much more with Delhi. Our focus is on intermediate cities, not megacities. We do want to invest in cities, and in fact, we even believe that urbanization is a must if we truly want to improve the lives of people. But we do not need people to go to a city which already has twenty million inhabitants.'

URBANIZATION LEADS TO GROWTH

The aforementioned focus on intermediate cities and belief that urbanization is a must, are the result of a recent paradigm shift of the Bank. After decades of almost exclusive engagement with India's rural areas, the Bank has now turned to urban regions.

'This is the result of a large comparative study the Bank conducted on the economic development of several large countries', Ruhl explains. 'We asked: What were the factors behind the economic growth in Brazil, China, the US, and the EU? What conclusions can we draw for India? Among other things, we found that urbanization plays a key role. We saw in all those countries that the faster a country urbanizes, the faster it grows. People in cities are more productive; they work harder to achieve their goals. That's not necessarily fun, but it is good for the economy. Urbanization also has a positive effect on the rural areas: with people leaving the countryside, agriculture has to become more productive. In sum, we found that if we want to eradicate poverty, we will need to start investing in urban areas.'

INTERMEDIATE CITIES

Ruhl explains what it is that makes cities so important for economic growth. 'It is where jobs are created. On top of that they are more efficient and cost-effective in provision of services than any other unity.' Mehta adds that both statements hold true in particular for intermediate cities. 'It is neither in the small towns nor in the megacities where jobs are created and where higher levels of service can be offered cost-effectively. It is in the newly created cities and in older emerging ones. So not in Mumbai and Delhi, but in Lucknow and Gurgaon, for example.' In other words: in the satellite cities of megacities, rather than in the core cities. 'This doesn't mean we should not try fixing the big cities also', Ruhl adds before we can ask the question. 'But it will be incredibly difficult and expensive to retrofit Mumbai and Delhi and it is definitely no quick-win scenario.'

RURAL IDEAL URBAN REALITY

At present about half of India's 1.2 billion strong population resides in cities. 'This number is even higher if you define "urban" by looking at population densities, instead of where official city borders start and end', Mehta says. It is expected that India's urban population will grow exponentially in the coming years and decades. 'Every year, ten million people move from the rural areas to the cities', Ruhl adds. 'Ten million! This process will continue for at least thirty years. We are talking about the biggest migration of people the world over. If we can ensure that these ten million people make a slightly better landing than they do now, you have a massive potential for improvement.'

One obstacle Ruhl and his team need to overcome, however, is the longtime reluctance among Indian policymakers to 'go urban'. Ruhl and Mehta explain that the legacy of Mahatma Gandhi still looms large in India when it comes to ideas regarding development. 'The traditional view has always been that India is a rural country. Gandhi stressed that the village is the ideal unit of development', Ruhl says. 'And this belief has become so ingrained that we found that even if you don't do what Gandhi did, you have to at least say what he said.'

URBAN DEVELOPMENT

The Bank's new orientation neatly fits in with what is currently one of its biggest projects in India: the Eastern Dedicated Freight Corridor. This is one of the two corridors which are heavily promoted by the Indian government. It is essentially a new freight rail track along an existing railway line running from Punjab in the northwest to Kolkata in the east. (The other corridor is called Western Dedicated Freight Corridor and goes from Mumbai to Delhi. This will be financed and built by the Japanese.) It fits because the corridor leads through some of India's least developed states and along several intermediate cities, such as Lucknow, Kanpur, Varanasi, and Allahabad. 'The government has now asked the Bank to do a study on how they can use the corridor as leverage for more efficient urban development', says Ruhl. 'The idea is to use the combination of a high population density, the transport corridor, and larger investments in those areas to push urban development. A very interesting idea, I think.'

One of the biggest obstacles in urban development in India is the absence of a government unit at the city level, Ruhl thinks. 'Normally a government levies taxes, and because you pay taxes you can ask for services. That mechanism doesn't work for Indian cities, as the governmental bodies are not located at the right level. There is the union; there are states, districts, and there are blocks. None of these are identical with the city. The result is that Indian cities have trouble organizing themselves, and their citizens have trouble holding them accountable.' When we note that Delhi is an exception, as it is simultaneously a state and a city, Ruhl emphasizes that this unique situation is purely a coincidence and not the result of a clear vision on how megacities should be governed.

WATER

A recurring theme in our discussions with Ruhl and Mehta on development in India in general, and in Delhi in particular, is water. The Bank worked on a major water project in Delhi in the past, but had to pull out of it prematurely. Ruhl explains: 'In 2005 we worked with the Delhi Jal Board, the waterworks. We attempted to reform the provision towards a public-private partnership, but protests forced us to stop the project. The protesters argued that the city, pressurized by the World Bank, was privatizing the water of the people. It became such a big deal that the bank stepped out of the project.'

The problems the public-private partnership project tried to address still persist. 'Water is a difficult sector', says Ruhl. 'Most people see it as God's gift, but in reality it is unbelievably expensive to get decent potable water all the way into someone's home. You keep pumping, and keep fixing pipes, but they keep falling apart because they are not paid for. At the same time it is a simple fact that piped drinking water is a lot cheaper than any alternative.' Adds Mehta: 'The main problem is trying to make people pay for the amount they use. Now they pay a flat charge. The moment meters are installed many people will end up paying less. In particular those who can least afford it, the poor. At present the poor pay far more to meet their water needs than I pay. I am ashamed of that each time I pay my monthly water bill.'

Ruhl and Mehta believe that Delhi can be an example to the world. They voice their approval of Debashree Mukherjee, former CEO of the Delhi Jal Board, 'We believe that if a system is rather corrupt, having the private sector involved is a solution. Mukherjee knew this. She also knows that politically this is a sensitive topic. So what she tried to do was using a few neighbourhoods as a demonstration model. To show the rest of the city that it works. We thought that was a great idea.'

24/7

There is one peculiarity with regard to water in India that Ruhl and Mehta want to make sure we know about. 'In India they have a phrase related to water that we haven't heard anywhere else, except in relation to retail shops: 24/7', says Ruhl. 'What is meant by it, is that it is impossible to supply water 24 hours a day, 7 days a week, and that there is something specific about India that it is not possible to do so.'

Mehta adds that Indians also disagree on whether supplying water 24/7 is a good thing at all. 'India is the only country where this question leads to a discussion. What is there to debate? Water should be made available to all, at all times. This is taken for granted in Uganda even! Yet in India the discussion continues and there is not a single city that provides it.'

He stresses that having water 24/7 is important and 'not merely a convenience or luxury'. 'There are many problems associated with not having it; health problems, for example. When you switch off the system it creates a vacuum in the pipes that draws bad water. You can imagine the potential problems created by contaminated water that flows from household taps the next morning, when the system is switched on again ...'

INDIA ARGUMENTS

Trying to change governance and supply structures in India is not easy, Ruhl and Mehta have found. Says Ruhl: 'Before we can achieve anything, we need to overcome feelings of "Don't tell us what to do". These are common in many developing countries and ex-colonies where we work. But India is a special case among these. We found that India and Indians are particularly proud and require a special approach. To be successful in presenting our agenda, our arguments need to be tailored to the local discourse.'

The discussion on climate change is a good example. Unlike most other countries where the World Bank is active, climate change is not listed as an aim in India. Says Ruhl: 'If we start whining too much that they need to change policies to save the polar bears, they will simply say "Sorry, but we don't have polar bears". So instead we argue: "India needs to grow fast, and to grow fast, India needs enough resources and water. Therefore, you need to be efficient with them." This analysis leads to exactly the same conclusion on what to do and what not to do as general arguments invoking climate change. Except when you say this to Indians, they will agree with you. As a bonus it fits perfectly in the Gandhian ideal of being frugal, of using your resources wisely. Thus, a whiney Western argument can be transformed to become an Indian argument. And if you want to convince Indians, the only way is to use an Indian argument.' With a smile Ruhl adds: 'To be honest, I have sympathy for that.'

SERVICES 12XW
ACE
ACE
ACE
ACE

ACE 14XW

DEDICATED FREIGHT CORRIODOR

27314
E.C.R.
VCD PROVIDED.
GMO
BP
FP

WORLD BANK INFRASTRUCTURE PROJECTS, INDIA

INDIA INTERNATIONAL CENTRE, DELHI

MY DELHI

ONNA RUHL

DELHI IS SPECIAL BECAUSE

There are several things that make Delhi special. First, it is only a city, but it is bigger in population than the entire Netherlands. Secondly, Delhi has an amazing number of historical sites. The city has been resurrected seven or eight times and you can find traces of all these in the city. I also think the phenomenon of urban villages within the city is quite amazing. The city expanded very rapidly, but you can still find these older nuclei, like Hauz Khaz and Shahpur Jat.

Compared to other cities, particularly Mumbai, Delhi is also special because of the number of cultural events. What is on display every other day is real art and not macramé.

THIS CAN BE IMPROVED

At present you can't speak about Delhi without talking about the safety of women. It is not the worst city for women, but it is the most well known. The city is not unsafe, but for women it is really unpleasant, particularly at night.

That is something you can improve quite a bit through planning, governance, and policing. The city should not have a bad reputation. That is important for the local women, but also in order to be attractive for tourists, which is in turn important for the city's economy.

MY FAVOURITE RESTAURANT

I'm a 'Beer and Kebab' man, yet I spend way too much time in fancy restaurants. Chonas in Khan Market is where I like to go when I get to choose. It is a canteen really. It is nothing special, but always crowded.

MY CHOICE OF TRANSPORTATION

Our Vespa. It is only slightly faster than the cycle, and in this city much faster than a car. Traffic is surprisingly structured, even though it may not seem like it. We drive between rickshaws and buses and because they drive on natural gas the pollution isn't so bad as one may think.

MY FAVOURITE DELHI BOOK

Each book in the five-book series *Empire of the Mughal* [written by Alex Rutherford] revolves around one Mughal emperor. I love reading about the Mughals and a lot of the history that is being retold in these books took place in this city. Traces of these events are still present. One day I read how Babur defeated the Lodhis, and the next I can actually visit the Lodhi tombs. Or, I learn how his son Humayun fell of the stairs in Purana Qila, and I can still visit these very steps. This gives a wonderful connection with the city.

MY FAVOURITE INSTITUTIONAL BUILDING

Either the North Block Complex, or the India Habitat Centre. The former is really India's presidential palace. It's stunningly beautiful. The latter I would select particularly for the roof of the atrium. That is such a marvel! Even in the worst heat it gives a good climate. I would say this roof is the Most Beautiful Thing in Delhi.

WHAT WE CAN LEARN FROM DELHI

We can learn from Delhi that we can modernize without having to give up the old. What is really very special is how they managed to project a metro system on such an enormously chaotic city. They made the plan, successfully executed it within time and within budget, and now they run it successfully. When you compare that to the Noord-Zuid Lijn [a large rail infrastructure project in the Netherlands] it is clear we can learn a lot from Delhi! The Netherlands has very wet soil, but the soil here isn't easy either. Still they did it within the deadlines and with respect for people who lived there. The key was a brilliant manager and support from the entire government. There was a solid financing model and an enormous focus.

MAKING SENSIBLE SURROUNDINGS

MOHAMMAD SHAHEER

Mohammad Shaheer (1948) studied Architecture and Urban Design at the School of Planning and Architecture (SPA), New Delhi, and Landscape Architecture at the University of Sheffield. From 1976 to 2003 he was on the faculty of SPA first as Professor and later Head of the Department of Landscape Architecture.

In 1980 he started his own firm, Shaheer Associates. Over the last four decades he has successfully participated in the landscape design of large public open space and heritage projects in Delhi, Lucknow, Kabul, Sriperumbudur, and Mecca. Shaheer also serves on national level government committees concerned with environment, conservation and city planning. He was a Member of the Delhi Urban Art Commission from 2005 to 2011.

He is deeply interested in writing on landscape and related topics. Together with Geeta Wahi Dua and Adit Pal, he recently edited *Landscape Architecture in India: A Reader* (LA, Journal of Landscape Architecture).

One sunny afternoon, we find ourselves in a remarkable residential complex in South Delhi called Zakir Bagh. The complex, designed by Raj Rewal in the late 1970s, was completed in the early 1980s. While listening to the famous landscape architect we came to meet here, we come to realize that it is no coincidence that his office is located right here in this very complex. Mohammad Shaheer admires Raj Rewal and will later say that for him one of the greatest joys of being a landscape designer is that it gave him 'the chance to collaborate with really fine architects'. Architecture, not landscape architecture, was his first love.

BECOMING A LANDSCAPE ARCHITECT

'It was the only thing I ever wanted to do', Shaheer says about studying Architecture at the School of Planning and Architecture (SPA) in New Delhi. 'I didn't have great philosophies or profound reasons as to why. I simply thought it would be something I could be good at.' Not in the least did he expect that it would lead to him becoming one of India's first landscape architects. 'In college we learned that architecture is about concrete, about statements and convictions. The landscape? That was at the very best just a background. To be honest, I thought that landscape architecture was all about writing the names of trees.' He laughs when he adds: 'You can understand it didn't sound like a very interesting activity to me'.

He explains how it was a scholarship that nevertheless made him end up working in landscape architecture. 'There were few good jobs to be found for graduate architects in Delhi when we were about to leave college in the early 70's. To travel and to study outside India was what everyone wished for, but scholarships to study abroad were scarce; at that time that was the only way one could imagine of financing one's studies. I was very fortunate that the School, after I had completed a postgraduate diploma in Urban Design, recommended me for a Ford Foundation Fellowship to pursue a Master's course in Landscape Architecture at the University of Sheffield. One of the conditions of the fellowship was that I would, upon returning to India, use this knowledge to contribute to the academic programme of the newly established Department of Landscape Architecture at the SPA. Faculty needed to be trained abroad, as there were no other courses in Landscape Architecture in India at the time. I was a good student, but even more important, I had fantastic teachers.'

Shaheer kept his promise to his alma mater, and quite a bit more than that. Upon completion of his two years in Sheffield, and a further two years in Northern Ireland gaining work experience, he returned to New Delhi to teach Landscape Architecture. He would do so for the next 23 years.

IMPROVING LANDSCAPE ARCHITECTURE EDUCATION

In the four decades since Shaheer was an architecture student, the scene has changed tremendously. Students in India can now choose to study Landscape Architecture at several different institutes. Also, there are about five to six hundred practising landscape architects. Progress indeed, but not yet enough, Shaheer feels. 'There's not enough professional work entrusted to landscape architects in the public realm, or integrated with infrastructure development.'

He thinks that there are at least two elements that course designers could add to current curricula to greatly improve them. The first is an introductory yet intensive course about Urban Design. His own early training in this subject has helped him throughout his career. 'Because I studied Urban Design my understanding of scale is good. That is something that many architects switching to landscape lack. The biggest difference between architecture and landscape architecture is scale. It is essential you develop that grip of scale in acres [rather than feet] to make sense of your surroundings, and to make sensible surroundings.'

The second element he would like to see added is a realistic introduction to the actual process of producing landscape architecture, and the speed required of landscape architects. 'Landscapes are conceptualised and developed to the implementation stage much faster than buildings are. As a landscape architect you have to cope with that', Shaheer says. 'Compared to landscape architecture, building architecture is a much more complex process. It is nowadays very technology-driven, and requires working with many consultants. A landscape architect can still be an artist; that's what attracts me to landscape design–the fact that you are not dependent on too many people.'

STYLE

Discussing various landscape architecture styles, Shaheer emphasizes that 'landscapes need not be "hard-edged"'. 'The current vocabulary of landscape architects, is often sharply angular, and with a tendency towards composition-making with lines and cuts. Sometimes there aren't even patterns. It might just be a bunch of lines with a few different colours.'

'There is more to Indian landscapes than our famous Mughal gardens. You have to go back in time to the long history before the two or three centuries of Mughal rule, and to the shorter but equally influential colonial period after.' Mughal gardens are famous for their water systems and the engineering. But Shaheer points out that they 'also display a particular genius in site planning'. 'This is very much a part of Indian landscape tradition', he says. 'In pre-Mughal literature gardens are described, and further information on what they looked like can be deduced from descriptions of the vegetation found at places of religion, the use of water in rituals, and the place of mountains, rivers and lakes as religious destinations. Its important to think of that symbolically; to embrace the power of the symbol, to think of gardens more as an experience than a form.'

'For example, you can compare this to the development of European and English gardens post-Renaissance, when landscape designers sought inspiration from antiquity, harking back to the myths and wisdom of ancient Greece and Rome. They took the visitors back to their own past–and attached them to it.'

OMNIPRESENT GRASS

Shaheer feels landscape architecture in India would not only improve when students' curricula are expanded, but also when professional architects and landscape architects take more time to educate themselves throughout their careers. 'We should read poetry-Kalidasa for example-and understand the references of our predecessors that literature records. It will give us a sense that there is more to the appreciation of the landscape than its aesthetics. It can bring us entirely new ways of looking at our work and materials.'

We ask him to give an example of how reading poetry has changed his outlook as an architect. The question, surprisingly, leads us to talking extensively about one of the prime materials of many contemporary landscape architects in India and abroad: grass.

'In landscapes all over the world it has become accepted that the soil be covered by grass. Even in my own designs this plant more often than not ends up playing a lead role. We should remain aware, however, that the choice for grass makes sense in many parts of the West, because it grows very well in the local temperate and wet climate, but that it is a silly idea that this should be applied everywhere in the world.'

Shaheer doesn't just want to make a popular environmental statement about grass needing too much watering in India's hot climate. His concern goes deeper. Studying Persian and ancient Indian landscaping traditions made him realize there is a problematic assumption underlying the contemporary omnipresence of grass: 'It has become an almost unchallenged rule in our field that grounds shall not be left bare at any time. The mantra has become that "soil needs to be covered to be good looking". But when I went back to the old sources, I found that although there was a lot of talk of courtyards, trees, and orchards, there was no discussion on grass and ground cover. From these texts and images I realized that the ground in and around the beautiful places our forefathers designed was not necessarily covered. It could be green with small seasonal plants growing on their own, or there could be nothing. It would depend on the season and leaving the ground visible was entirely acceptable.'

LINKING THE PARKS

During our time in Delhi, we hear Shaheer's name come up each time we discuss the intriguing plans of the Delhi Urban Art Commission (DUAC) to link the parks in central and other parts of Delhi through a green corridor. We ask Shaheer to tell us about it. 'It never really was a project, it was more an idea', he starts. 'During the time Charles Correa was the Chairman of the Urban Art Commission I was a member as well. We recognized that Delhi has this great benefit of having an amazing potential landscape structure. We have a river running north-south, and along it we have all these heritage buildings and landscapes: the Red Fort, the Old Fort, but also the Exhibition Grounds etc. On the west side we have another axis running north-south, the Ridge. In 1911 the middle part was filled in with Lutyens' New Delhi', with the addition of the Central Vista as a new axis from west to east.

'Lutyens was farsighted in making the Old Fort part of his setup, part of his Delhi. We know he looked at the map and tried to find out how this garden here and that garden there could be connected to create local networks. Almost a century later, we were working again on doing this connect: our plan was to design a number of green linkages integrating land-use, transport (especially the new metro) and existing open spaces to enhance access and environmental quality. It included a major west-east linkage, running virtually from Nehru Park via Safdarjung Tomb to Humayun's Tomb and the Yamuna beyond.'

Unfortunately the project has remained at the planning stage thus far. It has been exhibited, and the DUAC published it at the time; recently the idea was taken up by them again, but no action has occurred on the ground. Asked what is needed to make the plans a reality Shaheer says: 'What we really need is a landscape master plan which has some legality and agency.'

Yet, though drafted and designed at regular intervals, implementing master plans does not seem to be Delhi's forte, if we go by Shaheer's other tales of the city. He describes extensively how organized development over the past decades has always come too late. The bottom line being that 'whether allowed or not, people have to live, commerce has to go on with or without planning. Planning has hardly ever kept up with the urgent reality of people's needs. Master plans in Delhi seem to have been made mostly post factum, as an acknowledgement of all that has happened.'

FARMHOUSES

One type of architecture that has become synonymous with unplanned development and which is associated particularly with Delhi is that of the farmhouses. Shaheer explains the background of this type of building. 'In 1962 there was still quite a bit of rural land within and in the very close vicinity of Delhi. It was permitted to build small houses on this farmland, as farm-buildings, provided that you owned at least 2.5 acres. According to the rules and regulations this had to be a single-story dwelling of 1200 sq ft with a basement of a similar area for fodder-storage.'

'In the early years those who could afford it–the elite–bought this land and built these houses as weekend retreats. They might have built their houses a little larger, say 3,000-4,000 square feet but that would be it. Later farmhouses became larger and more luxurious, and the basement rule was easily forgotten. Houses of more than 10,000 square feet were built. Where the "bungalow" became to typify a style of living associated with colonial architecture, the farmhouse did so for the 80s and 90s.'

Shaheer alerts us to two important side effects of the farmhouse-trend; one positive and one negative. 'The negative long term effect has been that a large area of land contiguous with the "urbanisable" limits was lost to extremely low density, possibly wasteful, private development over the last thirty years or more. But on the other hand the projects did provide interesting creative opportunities for architects and landscape architects, myself included.'

He wishes for Delhi that those working on it would recognize that building and shaping cities is 'a huge responsibility'. 'It should not start and [should] not end–with business management', Shaheer says. 'Unfortunately the common prevalent attitude in India is that "doing quality landscape design" is associated with doing assignments for corporate clients, hotels, luxurious malls and large villas for the exclusive upper-end of society. But I emphasize, and have always emphasized that we should strive to do public works. In landscape architecture that is the biggest achievement: doing public works. If they are offering it to you, you should be proud and committed.'

RESPONSIBLE PUBLIC ARCHITECTURE

Two examples of public, responsible, and noble architecture that inspire Shaheer, and that surface again and again during our conversations, are the Sanskriti Kendra and the Nizamuddin Urban Renewal Initiative.

'O.P. Jain is the founder and owner of Sanskriti', Shaheer introduces the first. 'He chose to use his resources–the land in the farmhouse zone and his finances–in a restrained way. From 1982 onwards he has been engaged in making, and now maintaining, a cultural complex over an area of about 10 acres to house his private collections of terra-cotta, textiles, and antique everyday objects in a series of small museums within a serene and unobtrusive landscape setting. In this landscape he used aunobtrusive landscape setting. In this landscape he used a stone type familiar from landscapes and the ruins of monuments in and around Delhi. He inspired the development of an approach to construction, decoration and design around crafts and local techniques. In India its still possible to do this because the craft tradition is very much alive and available, if only we would encourage and use it. Whilst in many other countries examples of craftsmanship are to be found only in museums, we can still preserve and rejuvenate our traditions. Sanskriti Kendra is an example of a designed landscape that looks as if it has been found, not made. It is very local.'

The second example, the Nizamuddin Urban Renewal Initiative, started ten years ago. It is a partnership between the Aga Khan Trust for Culture and different sections of the Government of India, such as the Archaeological Survey of India, and the Ministries of Urban Development, Culture and others. The aim of the initiative is threefold: to improve the quality of life for the Hazrat Nizamuddin Basti community, to improve visitor experience for both tourists and pilgrims to the Humayun's Tomb–Hazrat Nizamuddin Basti area, and to restore the historical and architectural character of the monuments that stand there using traditional craftsmanship and materials.

The public component is the creation of an environmentally friendly, public open space. 'But', Shaheer emphasizes, 'apart from the aims and outcomes the interesting part of this programme is that throughout the focus is multidisciplinary: heritage conservation, renewal of traditional communities, social programmes, creation of recreational spaces ... they all come together in this initiative. On top of that it is very democratic, and not at all ivory tower-like. This project acknowledges the extremes in economic development in India, and challenges the conception that you can conserve and improve monuments and their environment without looking at the communities living around them. It thus challenges the starting point that monuments are merely decorations interesting for tourists. The people who live around them should have ownership to make a renovation successful. This project, in many ways, is something that is quite unique for India and truly something to draw lessons from.'

WORLD PEACE MEMORIAL, SOKA BODHI GARDEN, HARYANA

WORLD PEACE MEMORIAL, SOKA BODHI GARDEN, HARYANA

C. SANSKRITI KENDRA, DELHI

IMPROVEMENT OF THE PRECINCT OF THE MAZAAR OF MIRZA GHALIB AT NIZAMUDDIN, NEW DELHI. IMPLEMENTED BY THE AGA KHAN TRUST FOR CULTUR

IN COLLABORATION WITH THE ARCHAEOLOGICAL SURVEY OF INDIA AS PART OF THE NIZAMUDDIN URBAN RENEWAL INITIATIVE

LODHI GARDENS, DELHI

MY DELHI
MOHAMMAD SHAHEER

DELHI IS SPECIAL BECAUSE
Despite all the negative things we may say about this city, Delhi could actually be a model, an example, for the rest of the country when it comes to the process of city planning. It has a master plan. It also has the Urban Art Commission. Mumbai, and other cities in India, do not have an institution like that, nor any recognisable planning policy. There may be good things happening there, but they are the result of actions of individuals, not of policies and government bodies.

MY FAVOURITE PLACE
I have two: Lodhi Gardens and the India International Centre. Why? Perhaps because all the time I have been living here–almost fifty years now–they haven't changed much. You need places like that, anchors if you like, islands that encourage the comfortable illusion of stability; otherwise you'd be quite disoriented.

MY FAVOURITE RESTAURANT
The canteen of the Triveni Sangam. I love the atmosphere and the people there. It hasn't changed in all these years, and apart from having a good lunch, making a trip there gives me a chance to see the paintings exhibited.

MY FAVOURITE LANDMARK
I would say Khan Market. Or maybe better: the whole area around Lodhi Road. The garden, the streets and Khan Market: together they are a landmark, I think. The whole area gives the impression of civility in an otherwise very rushed and rude city.

READY FOR DEMOLITION
My first idea was some buildings around Connaught Place that were built in the 1970s. But more recently I have been quite unpleasantly surprised at what happened at Sikandra Road with the arrival of the over-ground metro there emerging in the centre of one of Lutyens' fine avenues. This used to be a very beautiful street providing access to Walter George's beautiful buildings for Lady Irwin College, and part of the Mandi House cultural hub. That is now lost.

MY FAVOURITE DELHI BOOK
I would recommend an interesting book on Delhi called *Trickster City: Writings from the Belly of the Metropolis*. It is written by Shveta Sarda and Azra Tabassum. It is about the people of Delhi. It takes you away from the general conversations about Lutyens' Delhi and into the lives of Delhi's masses and how do the majority of the people live in this city. It makes you look at the buses moving people around. It takes you away from the empty avenues of Lutyens', away from those 'masterpieces of design' and into the real Delhi.

WHAT WE CAN LEARN FROM DELHI
If you leave out the historical parts of Delhi, there is very little that can be learned from Delhi in terms of aesthetics. Granted, there are some beautiful areas, like the Diplomatic Enclave and Lutyens' Delhi, but the lessons they teach us are not that relevant for today. In fact, New Delhi's streets make me realize again and again that although intriguing, their design does not necessarily amount to a 'good plan'. Because of all those triangles and roundabouts you get lost very easily. Can you imagine, I have lived here for some 50 years, and I still get lost, especially while driving at night!

On the other hand, Delhi does show us that it's vital to be generous with provisions for infrastructure: roads, metro rail and open spaces. That is what people remember a city by. The avenues of Imperial Delhi function effectively almost a hundred years later. We will be fortunate if what is being planned today has a similar life-span.

Despite many flaws, Delhi continues to be a better planned and developed city than most other metros of comparable size, attracting many people from all over India in a largely inclusive social milieu. Lately it has become quite a dense city. Beginning in the last fifteen years or so the city has started to use land more effectively. That is something we can now learn too from this city.

DELHI: A VISUAL SPECTACLE

BAS LOSEKOOT

Bas Losekoot (1979) has a background in Graphic Design, Photography and Cinematography. He holds a BA in Photography from the Royal Academy of Art in The Hague. Currently he is completing an MA in Photography and Urban Cultures at Goldsmiths/University of London. His work has been exhibited at galleries, museums, and photo festivals worldwide. While still a student he was nominated for one of the most prestigious Dutch photography awards, the Silver Camera. In the years thereafter the list of nominations and awards grew; he bagged the Silver Camera Award in the category Foreign Documentary in 2011.

Nowadays Bas works as a documentary and portrait photographer. He has published his work widely and receives assignments from international magazines and advertising agencies. His passion, however, is street photography.

In his current project, called The Urban Millennium Project, he aims to capture life in the world's largest cities through his lens. He selected eight cities (New York, São Paulo, Seoul, London, Mexico City, Tokyo, Shanghai and Mumbai) based on their population size and density, the speed of their growth, and their geographical spread around the world. The eight city photo documentaries thus created will result in a single publication capturing the essence of twenty-first century urbanisms. For more information on the Urban Millennium Project, see: www.theurbanmillenniumproject.com

We met Bas Losekoot in 2012 at work in Mumbai. For this second volume we were delighted he accepted our invitation to join us in Delhi, to shine his light on and aim his camera at India's capital and its people. With the visit concluded and the photos selected, we asked him to share some of his thoughts on his experiences in Delhi.

PERSONAL AND PUBLIC SPACE

In addition to the wide streets, the heat, and the dust, Losekoot especially noticed that the concept of 'personal space' is defined differently in Delhi than in Europe. 'The high population density leaves you no choice than to encroach upon each other's space. Delhiites seem perfectly at ease with this. I found it fascinating to see how easily people interweave in the streets. People touch each other more. They stand closer together, and lean and hang on to each other in relaxed fashion. Men even walk around hand in hand. That's very different in the Netherlands, and most certainly in London, where I live now.'

It's not just personal space, but public space as well, that is defined differently in Delhi than in Europe, Losekoot feels. 'The very many informal businesses mean that life mainly takes place in the streets. Many shops and restaurants are in the open air, often in the most surprising places. Not a single patch of ground remains unused.'

BRUSH PASSING

This is an ideal environment for Losekoot to work in: in his work, architecture and urban planning often play an important role. In his Urban Millennium Project he is investigating how urban growth influences the human condition. 'As I go about taking my photographs for my project, I try to find answers to major questions: What is the ideal city? To what degree does urban development equal human development? What is the promise that a city holds?

He uses photography in an attempt to come to terms with the people in the streets and better understand them. 'I feel that gazes and gestures can reveal a lot about urban behaviour. I am attracted to places where people gather, brushing past one another in the street, and am intrigued by the human scale involved in urban architecture.'.

POLITICAL CITY

In many ways, Delhi was an easy place to work in, Losekoot thinks. 'A great deal is possible and people are very friendly and open.' Yet other aspects make it a difficult city to take photographs in. 'As a photographer, I adhere to the fly on the wall principle', he explains. 'I try to be as invisible as possible while working. This is impossible in a city like Delhi, and while sometimes this may have had a negative influence on the image, it does mean that the atmosphere is often good and you end up having interesting conversations.'

Another problem with regard to his work was the political nature of Delhi. 'As the political centre of India, it is a very bureaucratic city, with countless government officials, institutions, embassies and such. A lot takes place behind fences and railings, which of course is not very interesting in a photographic sense. Permission to enter compounds and buildings usually doesn't come overnight.'

LEARNING FROM

'My point of departure is that I want to approach 'Delhi is a visual extravaganza. So as a photographer, you need to be prepared for everything and to have thought out the technical aspects in advance. A good photo is often determined by the unexpected, which is why you have to trust your instincts and respond intuitively to whatever is happening. Delhi has taught me patience, and to feel at ease while standing still among all the clamour, in spots where everyone else is on the move. By relaxing and smiling, the most fantastic events can transpire, things you never had thought could occur beforehand.'

JAMA MASJID & LIGHT

Finally, we asked Bas what the photographic highlight of his visit to Delhi had been. Without any hesitation, he tells us it was Shah Jahanabad. 'Delhi is so very varied with regard to its huge population and architecture that I would have loved to stay here longer. I found the Jama Masjid area particularly interesting. It is so busy in the streets there. I had never seen anything like it: the crowds, the dust, the sweating, the racket, the sweet smells wafting past. And then, as the day draws to a close, that wonderful warm yellow and pink-tinged evening light falling through the streets... It's really incredible!'

- BLOCK
RENT
Shops/Office
9810119278
9910119278

HERO

दिल्ली मेट्रो प्रणाली मानचित्र एवं राष्ट्रमंडल खेल २०१० क्रीड़ा स्थल
Delhi Metro Route Map & Common Wealth Games 2010 Venue
Nearest Metro Station For Common Wealth Games Venue
24 X 7 DMRC Helpline - Dial: 011-128128
Security Control Room - Dial: 011-22185555

GLOBAL INDIAN ARCHITECTURE

SONALI RASTOGI

Sonali Rastogi (1967) graduated from the School of Planning and Architecture (New Delhi) and The Architectural Association (London) with a graduate diploma in Housing and Urbanism and a second graduate diploma in Design. She is Founder Partner of Morphogenesis.

Almost twenty years after it was founded Morphogenesis is the recipient of over 55 awards and has featured in over 350 publications, both national and international. The firm has been ranked several times among the Top 100 Architectural Design Firms worldwide by Building Design Magazine, UK.

Among its clients are Tata Housing, Reliance, Piramal Indiareit, L&T, Punj Lloyd, Ambuja Realty, Mahindra Lifespaces and the Intercontinental Hotel Group.

Rastogi regularly gives lectures and has been a part of various academic and design juries including The GRIHA Conference 2014, India Design ID 2013 Symposium and Trends for Architectural Excellence Awards, 2010.

She is also a founder member of Manthan; a cross-cultural creative platform for creative exchange, aiming to be a voice to the Indian creative community.

With around a hundred employees, seventy-five of whom are architects, Morphogenesis is one of the largest architecture offices in Delhi. Founders Sonali and Manit Rastogi set up the firm with a mission to take Indian architecture and design to what they call 'global platforms of discourse'.

ICONS

Rastogi feels that Indian companies have much more to offer than just merely being construction drawing and calculation back-offices. But internationally 'nobody is really looking out for Indian design or what is happening in India in terms of contemporary architecture', she has found. She illustrates this by telling about a lecture by a well known patron of architecture from the United States of America. 'He claimed no iconic architecture had been made in India in the past fifty years. He kept talking about how Indian design needs to take inspiration from the "iconocism" of the West. At the end of the lecture I felt offended', Rastogi recalls, 'and it was clear that good Indian architecture had not yet become visible to the global audience.'

It is not the word iconic in itself that she objects to. It is to 'the limited understanding of what iconic architecture is, to the idea that "iconocism" should be the most important kind of architecture around, and that an icon should be an icon everywhere, be universal'. 'However beautiful an iconic glass tower may be, it is an icon for there', she says. 'It is something that works in a cold climate, but not in Delhi, with temperatures hitting 47 degrees Celsius.'

MANTHAN

Rastogi thinks that underlying such disregard for what is happening in India is also the reality that India has yet to develop a strong discourse of its own. Trying to fill that gap, she and her partner started an initiative they called Manthan. 'It is a platform for conversation and discussion across various creative fields. The name is derived from Hindu mythology and means 'churning'. Manthan began when we asked eight people we only knew socially to come together one night. These eight people represented different professions: architects, writers, photographers, and artists. We told them that we found it remarkable that in Delhi, a city replete with cultural events, debate and discussion are missing.'

'That night we agreed we should organize events where people from different creative professions talk about the process of their work. It became a big success and fourteen such events were held in a span of three years' time.'

After three years and lots of interesting discussions we now want to make Manthan into a book. There have been a lot of requests to restart it, and soon it will and perhaps be open to public.'

FOREIGN STAFF

Exchanging ideas with non-architects through Manthan brought new energy to their work, and so does a multicultural work environment, Rastogi believes. 'Having people from all parts of the world working in the same studio changes team dynamics and ultimately enhances everyone's work.'

New policies, however, have made it increasingly difficult to hire foreign architects: a minimum salary requirement for foreign staff, but also new visa regulations. Says Rastogi: 'One problem is that visas are now given for short periods only. This means we invest six months teaching our working methodology and Indian specificities only to see them leave right after. The short period visas also make it difficult for foreign architects to see through an entire project from inception to completion.'

METHODS

Despite the increasingly restrictive policy environment, Morphogenesis still has some foreign staff. 'There is a clear difference in the way architects trained in Europe work and the way those trained in India work', Rastogi thinks. 'The first tend to work super-slow and super-accurate. They just do not do anything, do not take the next step, unless it is ab-so-lute-ly correct. Indian clients go completely mad working with them, because they are used to quick deliveries. The India-trained architect on the other hand, do fifty things at the same time, but inaccurately. They correct their mistakes as they go along. They come from a multitasking culture, and are used to working in a network of things going on simultaneously. They have jugaad, a term that translates to something like "We'll figure it out from whatever is available".'

Rastogi believes the secret to success lies in combining the two methods: 'The Western method of leaving some space to breath, slowing down, and doing it right the first time, works really well in combination with the Indian ability to produce a phenomenal quantity of work in unforeseen ways with a unique kind of resourcefulness.

For example, you can be a highly professional architecture firm with all processes streamlined, but the people who build your designs may do so in a seemingly very disorganized way. 'Modern day construction methodologies in India are only partially mechanized', says Rastogi. 'They are labour centric, and as a result in order to deliver a quality product the need for architectural intervention is quite high.' She explains that 'even if your process and documentation are immaculate, you will still get unexpected calls saying "This has gone wrong", "That has gone wrong". Europeans fall apart completely when this happens. They can't understand why this is happening, why somebody is saying that. They'll give an appointment to the person stating: "I'm busy now, please come back at so-and-so day and time". But by then ten other wrong things may have been built!'

The solution is to have the Western and Indian architects to complement each other. 'The Indian 'jugaad' will always be able to deal with the vagaries of the site. The Indian-trained architect will not let the project on the site collapse at any point and deal with everything that comes along from outside the office. The Western-trained architect will not let it go off track into other directions very easily. Together, it works wonderfully well.'

SUSTAINABILITY

Rastogi vehemently avoids Morphogenesis being categorized singularly as any kind of firm. 'If you must categorize us, just call us a process and result driven thinking practice'. But she agrees that hers is a firm with a focus on sustainability. Designing with a sense of responsibility for the environment is a hot topic for the studio, and our conversation keeps returning to it.

For example, when she tells about her own evolution. How she became interested in sustainability: 'From age 4 onwards I used to sketch buildings, mirroring what my father did, who was also an architect. Over time I converted from being a mostly visually inclined architect to one spending equal time thinking about sustainability. I now feel thinking in a sustainable and contextual way should be inherent to the design process and part of all the choices you make from inception to the details you choose.'

She shares how in a relatively short time she has seen 'thinking green' going from obscure to mainstream. She still remembers the days where a client would get green building certification because only then would he be able to get multinational corporates to lease the space. 'However today sustainability is understood as a beneficial way to approach energy consumption and it helps that there are financial and policy level incentives to do the same. Today as an attitude, going green is not that hard.'

GREEN BOOK

Yet another way in which Rastogi and her firm engaged with sustainable architecture is by demystifying the prevalent regulations and making them more accessible to common people. They redesigned the Green Architecture Book (*GRIHA*). The original is–to use Rastogi's words–an excellent technical document, but for laymen an 'excruciatingly painful' rule book. Their version is thin, light, and bright, with modern logos and an attractive layout. Nevertheless, it covers all the rules included in the big book. 'On the left page the information is presented for the client to understand, and on the right page is the checklist for the architect. We listed the various criteria, the scores given to them in the rating system, and whether or not they are mandatory. It is meant as a demystification of the rule set, but doesn't necessarily cover the whole green approach to architecture.' Rastogi hopes to publish it through a mainstream publisher in the near future.

BRITISH SCHOOL

When we ask for examples of successful sustainable Morphogenesis projects, their building for the British School in Delhi is the first thing that comes to Rastogi's mind. 'Here we planned to use treated sewage water in the schools for watering plants. However, they wanted to follow the British health and safety standards. In Britain the usage of such water in and around schools is not allowed, as children may come into direct contact with it. We said to them: "Being in India, where there is such a shortage of water, how can you not use water from sewage treatment plants?" and came up with a solutions to satisfy both requirements.'

'We proposed to apply a technique that is used in Dubai for crop irrigation in order to avoid evaporative losses: subsoil drip irrigation. Sewage treatment plant water is used, but we do not put it on the plant, but at the roots. It is a simple little tube line, which goes under the ground. They immediately agreed.'

STANDARDS

Another environmental plan Morphogenesis tries to push is that the comfort level of 22 degrees Celsius 'cannot possibly be universally applicable given the diversity in global climate'. 'At the same school we argued that there is no reason to have buildings for students 100% air-conditioned', Rastogi says. 'If they are properly shaded you can do without air-conditioning in some areas. And in those rooms where you do want to use it, we should ask ourselves why we follow worldwide standards and not set our own? Aiming for a temperature of 22 degrees indoors does not make sense when the outside temperature is 47 degrees Celsius. Such differences make you sick and are unpractical as they require you to carry an extra set of clothes to keep warm inside! Accepting this argument the school adjusted its standard to 26/27 degrees Celsius. The same story applies to international daylight standards, which are also 3-4 times higher than what is right for India, which has abundant daylight.'

Rastogi admits that some Indian rating systems have made efforts to adapt international standards locally. 'But they could be more consistent, she feels. 'The LEED [Green Building Rating System], for instance, modified some of its standards for the Indian context. At the same time they maintained other rules such as some regarding the use of certain machines. These rules worked perfectly for America, but they forgot that there weren't any machines like that here in India. The result: if we wanted to strictly follow the rules we would have to import those machines from America. This would obviously increase the carbon footprint like crazy! Similarly, LEED did not allow us to use a single air-conditioning system from India, because these did not meet the requirements developed to keep America green.'

NULLAHS

A Delhi project Morphogenesis has advocated has to do with and likes to tackle is to work with the city's natural drainage system: the nullahs. All over Delhi, these drains are used by slum residents as public toilets. Rastogi's partner Manit developed the idea to clean up the drains with local sewage treatment plants and combined this with ideas on urban mobility, urban design, and last mile connectivity. 'Once you have cleaned the nullahs and have made pathways along them, you will have a massive network of beautiful urban walking tracks connecting the entire city,' Rastogi explains. If that isn't enough, the plans could also be the long-sought ultimate solution to clean up the heavily polluted Yamuna river. 'The drains empty into the river. By treating their water locally, you ensure that what reaches the river doesn't become the unwieldy mass it is now. You also take away the need for mega schemes devised to clean up the Yamuna that don't address the roots of the problem and hence are mostly wasteful.'

Their plans received a lot of attention from media and press, and a variety of government bodies asked them to take part in panels and discuss it. Yet, so far, they remain paper plans. 'As with a lot of things in India, there is a quagmire of numerous authorities responsible for these nullahs, and nobody clearly knows who has to do what. We hope it doesn't lose steam and one day we are able to give back to the city of Delhi a clean nullah system.'

PEARL ACADEMY OF FASHION, JAIPUR

GYS VISION, GURGAON

MARBLE ARCH, UPPAL HOUSING, CHANDIGARH

DS GROUP FACTORY & OFFICES, NOIDA, DELHI

MY DELHI

SONALI RASTOGI

DELHI IS SPECIAL BECAUSE

For at least two reasons Delhi is a very special place to be at present. First, many paradigm shifts are happening currently. A new Indian global culture and a new contemporary Indian architect are coming into being. Secondly, projects in this city come at every level: from the highest end of luxury that the world has ever seen, to projects for residents who are living below the poverty line. That bandwidth may not exist in many places. Because of these reasons New Delhi today is a very exciting place to practise architecture.

THIS CAN BE IMPROVED

There should be more professionalism. It will inevitably bring about a better built environment. The general public should have more awareness of the built environment. It will make for a greater demand for better architecture. Architecture education should be updated. It will produce better architectural discourse, which would then produce better architecture.

MY FAVOURITE RESTAURANT

Delhi has such good food. When I get friends from abroad I take them to Pandara Road Market; sometimes even straight from the airport! There are several traditional Indian butter chicken restaurants, serving what is considered to be the best butter chicken in the world. I love street food and the golgappa's and chaat at Evergreen are my favourite.

MY FAVOURITE LANDMARK

Delhi's trees. It is a very green city and the trees, their types and sheer numbers, are very unique. Here I am, the Outer Ring Road not even 150 feet away, and yet I feel like I'm sitting in my own heaven!

MY FAVOURITE DELHI BOOK

What my favourite Delhi book is changes all the time. I come across interesting things, which then become my favourite for the moment. At present it is, for example, a book with maps of Shahpur Jat, maps about how people use the area. A constant favourite is The Trees of Delhi by Pradeep Krishen. I love it and think it is really what people need. I have gifted it to maybe a hundred people already.

READY FOR DEMOLITION

So many big structures. Those old structures, where they simply put some blue glass on for a "modern look" to increase their rental value. Delhi itself doesn't have so many of these, because of certain regulations. But when you are anywhere around Delhi you see a lot of those senseless coloured glass fake sort of facades.

MY FAVOURITE DELHI FILM

Rang De Basanti. I like it because it talks about change. It talks about young people who hang out together without the typical gender stories. Youth, love, revolution, communal agendas and history are all depicted with in the format of the dance and music that is deeply embedded in the Indian Cinema culture. They talk about inhibitions between and amalgations of Hindus and Muslims. The film depicts the marked cultural difference between Old Delhi life and Central Delhi life, whilst an understated commentary on contemporary Delhi forms the underlying theme.

MY FAVOURITE BUILDING

Three buildings we designed: the India Glycols Corporate Office on the Greater Noida Expressway and the DS Group Factory & Offices, currently under construction in Noida.

WHAT WE CAN LEARN FROM DELHI

How differences coexist. Mumbai is diverse as well, but as a city it has a singular drive: to be commercially viable. Delhi has many different influencing factors that coexist. People come to Mumbai to become a Mumbaikar. People come to Delhi and to form their own little communities. Even while living in this megacity they maintain their cultural identity and don't entirely get absorbed into a larger culture. In that sense Delhi has cultural diversity and it's own uniqueness in co-existing. Delhi is a microcosm offering a window into time from centuries of evolution.

BUILDINGS ARE NOT ETERNAL

MADHAV RAMAN

Madhav Raman (1978) graduated from the School of Planning and Architecture, New Delhi as an architect. In 2001, together with Vaibhav Dimri, he started Anagram Architects in New Delhi. The young practice has garnered much international acclaim including a nomination for the Aga Khan Award 2010 and inclusion in the *Wallpaper** magazine's 'Architects Directory 2009'. Recently, they were included in AD50, The Architectural Digest Magazine's list of the 50 most influential Indian designers of 2014.

Anagram presently consists of nineteen staff members and holds a diverse portfolio. Projects encompass public infrastructure planning, urban design, architecture, sceneography, broadcast design, furniture design, and interior design. The firm is committed to deeply contextual designs that encourage sustainable lifestyles.

In addition to his design, advice and consultancy work within Anagram Architects, Raman is also associated with his alma mater, the School of Planning and Architecture, New Delhi, where he conducts a design studio and guides students on their dissertations. Raman frequently lectures on architecture, urbanism, sustainability and non motorized transit at other institutions in India as well, among which the Indian School of Business (Hyderabad) and the CEPT University (Ahmedabad).

Now twelve years old, Anagram is coming of age. They recently moved into a new studio, adopted a new logo, created a new webpage, and, most significantly, are about to restructure the entire firm. 'When we started we didn't have a philosophy of any substance', explains Madhav Raman, one of the two partners who founded Anagram. 'But now, twelve years on, me and Vaibhav [Dimri] do have very strong opinions on what we do. This made us feel the need to create a bit of distance between the various types of work we do, between our architectural work and our consultancy and advisory work, and to restructure ourselves into a firm with three different arms, rather than have all aspects united within one company.' Creating this distance is particularly crucial in order to maintain the integrity of their architectural practice, Raman feels. 'If ethical conflicts arise from projects done by clients that used us as a consultancy, then the responsibility for those conflicts should be transferred to those clients.' After a brief pause he adds: 'We want to protect what we think and what we believe in from what we might be arm-twisted into.'

CONSULTANCY

Raman explains the role the consultancy wing of their firm shall play. 'When we started, we found that as a small young office that had won a competitive design bid for a private project, we didn't have the bandwidth to deliver on the consultancy aspects of the work we were offered. It is impossible for any small and young firm to do so. As a result, small companies are practically forced to associate themselves with a senior architect, who then takes their design. At Anagram we want to fill that gap for smaller firms, and lease our consultancy services to them. But our idea is that our consultancy would operate entirely independent from how we practise our architecture.'

ADVICE

The restructuring should also lead to a capitalization of advice now often given for free. 'Many of our clients, especially larger and more corporate clients, recognize that we know a fair bit about the existing master plans. They then lean on us for more information and guidance. "Does acquiring this plot of land make sense?" "Will the numbers add up, five or ten years from now?" "Will this plan of ours violate any laws?" The questions keep coming. A lawyer will simply chart out ownership issues, a real estate consultant can enlighten them on the speculative value of the land now and after construction. But none of them can tell them whether the project as a whole makes sense. As architects, we are able to give the right kind of holistic advice that includes the legal, the business, the design, and even ethical aspects.'

'In other cases we dole out advice on the proposed programme of projects, the ideal financial structure, the number of phases required and how to ideally pace things', Raman continues. 'Taking and giving free advice on all those aspects is common in this industry. But how often is it genuinely free advice? How often does the information provided by an architecture firm lead a potential client to consider that firm, even though it might not be the best one for the job? I think that's unethical. Just as it is equally unethical to expect architects to invest lots of time, yet give free advice.'

ARCHITECTURE

As architects, Anagram's best-known project is their office building for the South Asian Human Rights Documentation Centre in Safdarjang Enclave Extention in New Delhi. Their design, and in particular the brick façade, gained Raman and Dimri national and international recognition as architects. 'It was a small office building', Raman says. 'It was located on a busy corner. We sought an appealing way to block sounds and sights from the street. We decided on using a masonry wall with rotated bricks allowing for ventilation and daylight.' The result? A stunningly beautiful brick wall.

AWARDS

Completed in 2005, the building won the young architects the prestigious Architectural Review Emerging Architecture Award in 2007. 'By then it was already really a finished project for us, a project of the past', Raman says. But after receiving the award the project more or less came to life again; they started getting emails from various publications and organizations about it. Soon, as Raman puts it, 'even stranger things started happening'. They were asked to submit their building to compete for awards, and subsequently won them. 'We were quite surprised at the traction this building was creating for us. We found it kind of amusing also, as it made us aware of the huge importance given to being recognized as an award-winning architect.'

VOLLEYBALL

Marketing-savvy as they were, they made a little media package, and emailed it around. The internet got hold of it. The way it was used made them realize that internationally there is 'very little critical editorial thinking in any of this'. 'It reminds me of a game of volleyball', says Raman, 'except the ball is not in the same court. You kick the ball here. He bounces it. It goes there, there, and there. It grows bigger and bigger and bigger. Then one day you read about your own project and you hardly recognize it!'

The further from the building they got, the more their practice seemed to be identified with the 'brick building'. 'We are perfectly happy when people celebrate it. We really like that building. But I don't think it represents us beyond a certain moment in time.'

This pragmatic attitude is underlined by Raman telling us rather matter-of-factly that the façade of the building is currently no longer entirely the one designed and built by them. 'The owner of the building put doors in it', he says. 'No, that doesn't bother me. I have the pictures. During a project it is a pain when they do not value your opinion and they question the integrity of your design. But after completion … the building should be relevant for the user, or for the real estate developer who wants to sell it. I can't get sentimentally attached to my buildings. When I design them I know they won't be eternal.'

LIABILITY

Our talk on restructuring Anagram as a three-armed firm led us to discuss a peculiar feature of practising architecture in India with Raman: the fact that architects are supposed to have unlimited liability during the construction phase. 'That is true', Raman says when we ask whether architects in India indeed are required to carry such a burden. 'We are liable for anything that the firm does. Suppose we cause a loss to our client and the client takes action against us, then our architectural licence basically means we have unlimited liability in both civil and criminal cases. In other words, if said client successfully sues us to recover costs, then Vaibhav and my personal assets are up for grabs.'

Raman explains that the laws governing practising architecture have not kept up with the reality of construction in India. 'In the out-dated regulations it is assumed that if someone wants to build, they usually own the land, and have the resources to construct a building. Following this scenario, they will hire an architect and the architect would be the top of the project. Everyone would listen to him or her. But that's not how it works anymore, if it ever did. Post 1992, post the liberalization of the economy, we saw the emergence of the developer. In that scenario the land is owned by someone, the capital comes from somewhere else, and the building is made for again someone else. All kinds of other professionals have become part of the process, but licences have not kept up.'

The architects' liability is unlimited until the time a completion certificate is issued by the municipal authorities. At that point the liability transfers to the client.

FUTURE

Looking around the massive space of their new office, we ask which unusual projects Raman and his partner have lying on their desks currently, and what they dream of occupying their office and minds in the near future.

The Ring (T)Rail Urban Renewal Project is an example of the first. 'There is a railway line, the Ring Rail, which circles Delhi, but is now hardly used. Our plan is to rework this railway into a 35.3-kilometre-long pedestrian and bicycle-friendly corridor. We want to add one more programme to it though: street commerce. We want to work with street vendors to create a cooperation for them, so that they can benefit from collective health care and such like. And we think the Ring Rail can be a perfect place to showcase and celebrate that important aspect of Indian life: commercial street culture.

As for their dream project, Raman doesn't need to think long. He would like to build a good school. 'Intellectually I will find designing a good school very interesting because of the kind of spiritual configuration, the ideas, the sense of what it is,' he says. 'Over here [in India] all of us went to school sitting in these cages. The schools in this country are very badly designed, like cell blocks. That, while there are so many exciting things you can do. For example, devising designs that merely by occupying them can be used as a teaching tool. We realized that spaces can be smart.' 'These are not unique ideas', Raman adds modestly, 'but the chance to articulate them through our designs will be exciting.'

SOUTH ASIAN HUMAN RIGHTS DOCUMENTATION CENTRE (SAHRDC), DELHI

KINDRED HOUSE, DELHI

KINDRED HOUSE, DELHI

ANAGRAM OFFICE, DELHI

FOOD LABYRINTH, DELHI

MY DELHI
MADHAV RAMAN

DELHI IS SPECIAL BECAUSE

Delhi is where I grew up. It is the only city that I can really say that I know inside out. I can imagine myself living everywhere, but Delhi is definitely home.

THIS CAN BE IMPROVED

Delhi has a huge inferiority complex. Unnecessarily. The biggest thing that Delhi can do to improve is to appreciate itself in every sense: its people, its spaces, its buildings, the good and the bad. Too many people are cynical about this city, but I feel that Delhi is an opportunity, if you want to see it.

MY FAVOURITE PLACE

My favourite place in Delhi is the Ridge. I live right next to it. It is also nice that you have these really secluded pockets in the middle of Delhi. I guess what appeals to me are these places, edges, where you can go in and out of the city quickly.

MY FAVOURITE RESTAURANT

Generally I prefer to eat at home, and I don't have one favourite restaurant. I have seasonal favourites. Right now Chez Nini in Meher Chand Market is one of my top picks. They serve really good French-Canadian food. And I have recently added Cafe Lota at the National Crafts Museum to my list of favourites. They serve quaint and lesser known Indian preparations which have the ability to yank out childhood memories from the back of your mind!

MY FAVOURITE LANDMARK

The New Delhi Railway Station. Even though I grew up in Delhi, my family originally comes from South India. We would spend our summer holidays in Chennai. These holidays would start at the station. School would be closed, and next came the station with its particular sounds, smells. The station would also be the context when the realization would hit me that the summer was over and it was time to go back to school.

READY FOR DEMOLITION

Gurgaon. Gurgaon is wrong in all sorts of ways. Right from its inception, the reasons why Gurgaon was started, up until what you see there today; there is nothing to like about it. It does not have a sewage system. It does not have public transport. There is no basis for it to exist other than real estate. It has been developed in a manner in which it cannot be improved unless you literally demolish everything and start again from scratch.

MY FAVOURITE DELHI BOOK

I have two. Pradip Krishen's *The Trees of Delhi* and a book for children illustrated by Anita Balachandran about Humayun's Tomb (*Let's Explore Humayun's Tomb*, text by Narayani Gupta). It is a very, very beautifully illustrated book and tells the little stories behind the monuments of Delhi.

WHAT WE CAN LEARN FROM DELHI

Acceptance. You come to accept strange things in Delhi. You realize that in Delhi the most bizarre things are possible. Sometimes they are good things, sometimes they are bad. You will stop thinking here that you can 'solve' Delhi. You can't. I can't. Delhi can't be solved. You can't solve a city, and cities should not be solved. The city should be lived there and enjoyed. Only when you start doing that–enjoying it, living it–will it start shining for you. Too many people working on the city, urbanists, others, are cynical. They don't see Delhi as an opportunity. There is so much potential if you would just be joyful about the city.

LONG-TERM SCENARIOS ON FOUR-WHEEL PUSHCARTS

ANNE FEENSTRA

Anne Feenstra (1967) studied Architecture at Delft University of Technology. He worked with Will Alsop in London before he established his own studio, AFIR Architects, in 2004. He has been working and living in South Asia for the past decade. He taught architecture at Kabul University, at the School of Planning and Architecture, Delhi, and at Tribhuvan University in Kathmandu. In 2009 he established arch-i, a platform for architecture and urban planning. Acknowledged for his inclusive architecture in which he collaborates with local communities and craftspeople, he became a Laureate of the Global Award for Sustainable Architecture 2012 in Paris. Feenstra did his first design-and-build project in Nepal in 2013, and recently set up Sustainable Mountain Architecture in Kathmandu in 2014.

Together with a dedicated team of young Indian architects and designers, Dutch architect Anne Feenstra began a unique journey in 2009. Rather than chasing architecture assignments, he started chasing answers to questions he heard himself ask each time he would simply look around in Delhi. Questions like: Why do the majority of infrastructure and architecture projects in India lack durability, sensibility, and sustainability in their design and execution? Why are the skills and knowledge of the very good architects, very good planners, and very good landscape architects that are available in India seldom used? Where are the cities in India heading? What will happen to them if nothing changes?

ASKING QUESTIONS IN TWELVE CITIES

To find answers to these and other questions, Feenstra and his team started touring India. In 2009–2010, in collaboration with the Amsterdam Centre for Architecture, (Arcam) they visited twelve Indian cities. They criss-crossed the country: from Chandigarh to Chennai, and from Goa to Guwahati. 'We took the Arcam exhibition as a starting point. It highlighted successful Indian urban projects of the past 25 years and in some cities local architects were asked to reflect on the future 25 years as well.

'These talks inspired us to organize panel discussions where the audience was invited to think aloud what their city would look like in twenty-five years' time if business was to carry on as usual', Feenstra says. 'We pushed the discussions towards possible course corrections and asked how the public would like to go about implementing these corrections for their own cities.'

Inspired by these interactions, and by other long-term scenarios such as the Dutch government's Randstad 2040, Feenstra decided to continue his quest in the city he knows best: Delhi. This was the start of Delhi 2050, an ongoing project. Says Feenstra: 'My wife and I live and work a part of the year in Delhi. We have friends and family here. We look at current developments and the direction the city is heading and we deeply worry about the city, about its future, about its liveability.' He picked 2050 instead of 2010 because he thought that for Delhi it would be a better year to look at. 'When people hear that number they start calculations in their minds: "Will I still be around?" That thought alone can actually provide more boldness in creative thinking.'

LONG-TERM SCENARIOS

The purpose of Delhi 2050 is to 'fundamentally rethink the long-term future of the capital of India'. To that end, Feenstra and his team set out to create an extensive local and international network. Over the year,s architects, academics, educators, educational institutions, planning offices, and other government bodies were involved in the project and asked to provide input to various–as Feenstra refers to them–'long-term thinking scenarios'.

He explains: 'For one such scenario we asked for example what could happen if we were to use all our innovative ideas and the powers of design to re-value the street. In India streets are traditionally used in so many more ways than merely as a path to travel on from A to B. Streets are also sites for religious and wedding processions. And all kinds of trades and service men have their workspaces on the streets; think of vendors, 'press wallahs' (the people who iron clothes), cobblers, ice-cream vendors etcetera. Cars increasingly claim this space. They engulf the city. Every day approximately a thousand new cars are added to the streets of Delhi!'

LIFE STREET MODEL

One of four long-term thinking scenarios Feenstra and his team thus came up with for Delhi is the Life Street Model. It reminds us of Jane Jacobs' pioneering ideas on street life. 'This model celebrates the value of empty spaces between buildings, while at the same time it accepts and accommodates for cars and other motorized transport', Feenstra explains. 'If this model is followed, we hope to see gated communities disappear and the "right of way" reappear.'

Together with three other such models, a physical representation of Delhi 2050's Life Street Model was placed on a four-wheel pushcart, the type of cart normally used by vegetable sellers. 'We toured the streets of Delhi for ten days with these carts. It was absolutely fantastic to see the response of the common man and to listen to their remarkable interpretations and ideas. Architects and planners in India usually do not talk with the people they design their long-term plans for. We did, and we believe those dialogues produced better solutions, and enhanced a local sense of ownership regarding our plans.'

DWARKA TEST SITE

Feenstra explains that after taking the project abroad to various exhibitions, the next step for them was to find a test site to demonstrate the ideas gathered and developed so far within the Delhi 2050 framework. They selected the southwest Delhi neighbourhood of Dwarka. 'Designed for 1.2 million people in the 1980s, Dwarka today is only half-built and faces the dramatic challenge of not having enough water. We took panels with info graphics and possible design solutions to Dwarka. It was an unforgettable experience, and not just because the monsoon poured down a stunning 60 mm of rain that day. We had great interactions with angry inhabitants. They shared their frustrations about the water supply. They were furious since all that precious rainwater that we saw coming down would disappear via storm drains. Not able to use it, they would instead be forced to buy expensive and poor-quality saline water from water tankers the next day.'

Feenstra and his team shared the ideas and recommendations of the Delhi 2050 network with the citizens of Dwarka. 'They got interested since they saw we wanted to find solutions for them. They enthusiastically joined us in erecting experimental public art installation of words like 'WATER?', 'SAFE', 'WALK!', and 'PEOPLE'. We wanted to place some fundamental issues on the agenda with these words.'

The team is happy with the outcomes of the first phase of Delhi 2050. Says Feenstra: 'I believe that we must have reached an audience of close to 75,000 people through radio and internet messages. Subsequently, many housing societies expressed their interest in what we are doing and three of them approached us to design a self-sufficient water management system for them that includes water harvesting.'

ARCHITECTURE

Talking enthusiastically and extensively about arch-i's efforts to research and improve the city of Delhi, we could almost forget Feenstra is an architect, with two architectural firms to run as well: AFIR (Anne Feenstra Ideas Realisation) and SMA (Sustainable Mountain Architecture). AFIR was established in 2004 in Amsterdam, but it moved to Kabul, Afghanistan in the same year, where Feenstra started teaching at the University of Kabul. After several small residential projects, larger projects followed, such as Maternity Waiting Homes for UNICEF, the Visitor Centre, Gate House, and Bazaar for the National Park in Bamyan, and the renovation of the National Museum in Kabul. 'In 2010 and 2011 we started getting some architecture assignments in our Delhi office as well, while in Nepal we decided to only do architecture projects with our SMA team', Feenstra explains.

When we ask what drives him in his architectural work, Feenstra says he finds little inspiration in contemporary architecture or contemporary architects. 'The Bengali writer and philosopher Rabindranath Tagore, critical theorist Erich Fromm, the stories of Sufi Mullah Nasruddin, bio-agriculturalist Masanobu Fukuoka, and the work of artist Julie Mehretu ... all those non-architects have a deeper impact on my understanding of the world than the work of the so-called star architects. Most of the star-architect buildings are so exclusive that they actually resent people. They exclude. The users of their spectacularly expensive buildings are actually regarded a nuisance; they mess up the perfect spatial perspectives.'

COMMUNITY-BASED ARCHITECTURE

Learning from peers is one strategy Feenstra adopted to overcome obvious obstacles in working in India, such as those related to implementation. 'Apart from internal discussions, we had long talks with architects like Revathi Kamath and Bijoy Jain. They have, in my opinion, been able to design and build very well in India. We decided in India as a team to focus on community-based projects, where it is possible to combine locally available building material and skills of local craftsmen with contemporary and innovative ideas. Our focus is mainly on rural areas for now. We have successfully completed projects in Sikkim, Himachal Pradesh, and Ladakh. Building at 4200 metres altitude, like we did in Ladakh, is a thrilling experience. But we certainly have the ambition to build in Delhi as well.' Laughing he adds: 'Who knows, maybe by 2050 that will happen.'

LEARNING FROM

Before we leave Feenstra wants to share a final valuable piece of advice: 'If you want to work in India as a foreigner, always keep in mind that upon arrival in Delhi at Indira Gandhi International Airport, at immigration the first row for foreigners is number 27. Most visitors, who come for a piece of the pie of emerging market opportunities, forget that, in the long run, in India modesty is a must. Rather than imposing master plans, exclusive built environments, gated residential communities, and privately developed infrastructure, we should take a deep breath, use our powers of observation, and see what we can learn from Delhi.' We couldn't agree more.

MIDDLE SCHOOL FOR KARGYAK, KARGYAK IS AN ISOLATED VILLAGE SITUATED IN THE INDIAN HIMALAYAS IN THE ALTITUDE OF 4200 M ABOVE SEA LEVEL

MIDDLE SCHOOL FOR KARGYAK, KARGYAK IS AN ISOLATED VILLAGE SITUATED IN THE INDIAN HIMALAYAS IN THE ALTITUDE OF 4200 M ABOVE SEA LEVEL

ARCH-I IN ACTION ON THE STREETS IN DELHI

DL9S AH 2952

LOTUS TEMPLE, DELHI

MY DELHI
ANNE FEENSTRA

DELHI IS SPECIAL BECAUSE
Delhi is a real melting pot. People from all over India and South Asia have created the unique cultural richness of the capital. Delhiites come from Uttarakhand, Punjab, Kashmir, Kerala, Tamil Nadu, Bihar, West Bengal, Sikkim, Nepal, Tibet, Afghanistan, and Bangladesh. And they all bring their culture with them. Unfortunately, not everyone realizes what a blessing this really is for a city, as it seems easier for some to speak the anti-immigrant language.

THIS CAN BE IMPROVED
Public space and public art in Delhi are in bad shape. A lot of work needs to be undertaken in the years ahead to improve this. As for public art, I find the stainless steel sprouts artwork by Vibhor Sognani at the AIIMS Flyover a rare positive example. With arch-i we have actually held workshops and picnics there. We were sitting in the midst of the traffic produced by the 46 million people of the National Capital Region. With regard to public space I hope that the reduction of these areas can be stopped and that the massive water, sewage, and air pollution problems will be taken seriously by the government. With Delhi 2050 we hope to contribute to that process.

MY BEST PLACE TO RELAX
Understanding by sketching relaxes me anywhere in Delhi. Be it in Chandni Chowk or at the Lotus Temple.

MY FAVOURITE RESTAURANT
The best Bihari kitchen in town called Potbelly is my favourite restaurant in Delhi. This restaurant opened its doors in August 2011 in Shahpur Jat and has served authentic Bihari food ever since. I love the *litti* (ball-shaped snacks made of wheat and lentil flower), *sattu* (a mix of ground pulses and cereals), and *baingan ka bharta* (an eggplant dish).

MY CHOICE OF TRANSPORTATION
I use the Metro and love it. I think Delhi can consider itself lucky that visionary people realized the power of 'travelling public'. That is not an existing phrase but I like it better than talking about 'public transportation'. We are humans, we want to travel, not be transported.

It is impressive that within one decade, by 2015, Delhi's Metro network will have the same length as 80% of all the Paris metro lines combined. But the Metro is far from flawless. You had better not look critically at how the metro stations are integrated in the city fabric. It is awfully disappointing. And that while the quality of infrastructural interventions can have such a huge effect on the city's built environment. It is one of those projects that made me wonder: Why would the government not include skilled designers from different backgrounds in a project like this? If they did they could drastically reduce the long-term costs of the Metro infrastructural system.

MY FAVOURITE LANDMARK
Apart from the obvious semi-public Habitat Centre, we have, at walking distance from our Camp (that is what we call our arch-i office), the Lotus Temple. Almost as difficult to build as Jorn Utzon's Sydney Opera House, the Temple has an obvious iconic value. The internal acoustics and the flow between building, landscape, and water are done very well.

READY FOR DEMOLITION
Rather than demolishing something I think it is important to find contemporary ways to continue the Indian tradition of re-using materials. Increasing impatient capital combined with non-accountability results in demolishing and dumping material anywhere

MY FAVOURITE DELHI BOOK
Anupam Bansal's *Architectural Guide Delhi*. The book provides deep insights into Delhi's contemporary architecture and how the fabric of the city came about.

MY FAVOURITE DELHI FILM
The Latent City by Krishnendu Bose. He made this documentary in 2009 and, as he puts it himself, 'urges us to re-imagine the future of Delhi, through the eye-glass of public art'. It never went to the larger public, but it won awards at various festivals.

THE DELHI METRO

WORKSHOP AT THE SCHOOL OF PLANNING AND ARCHITECTURE

Delhi Metro at a glance. In 1998 the construction of the Delhi Metro started. It was in a different city than where the first plans were drawn for fourteen years earlier: the population had doubled and the number of vehicles on the roads had risen fivefold.

Construction went ahead at top speed and after only four years the first trains began plying between Shahdara and Tis Hazari on part of the Red Line. Six more lines followed, the last to open being the the rail connection to the Delhi Airport: the Delhi Airport Express Line.

Currently the network has a total length of 193 kilometres. There are 146 stations of which 38 are underground, five at-grade, and the rest elevated.

Trains run daily between 04:40 AM until midnight. At peak frequency they come with an interval of merely three minutes. On an average day 2.4 million trips are made. Of the six lines, the Yellow line (Jahangirpuri to HUDA city centre) and Blue line (Dwarka Sector-21 to Noida City Centre/Vaishali) see most passengers.

WORKSHOP: MOBILITY IN DELHI

On 19 November 2014, we–Gert Jan and Pelle–met with students of the School of Planning and Architecture in New Delhi for a day-long interactive session with the overarching theme Mobility in Delhi.

After the formal kick-off by Mandeep Singh, Head of the Department of Architecture of the School of Planning and Architecture, we started the day with a few short presentations. Arch-i gave a brief introduction to their previous and current work, under the heading Delhi 2050 (see page 183). Madhav Raman of Anagram Architects presented their plans for revitalizing the Delhi Ring Railway: the now mostly redundant 35-kilometre circular rail network that runs parallel to the Ring Road. Gert Jan presented a case study of the Bijlmer mobility hub in Amsterdam, while Pelle explained the background of *Learning from Delhi*.

Following these talks, the focus shifted to the Delhi Metro: the almost 200-kilometre long rail network that since just over a decade connects almost all parts of the city. Students then formed smaller groups to discuss the Metro's various functions in and effects on the city and its inhabitants.

RAJIV CHOWK

The most obvious effect of the Metro on the city, apart from reduced travel times between many places, is the physical appearance of almost 150 metro stations. It changed large tracts of the city's landscape. But did these structures add value to the city beyond their main function as transport locales? The students presented Rajiv Chowk station (Connaught Place) as an example of a metro station that has enhanced the available public space. 'The roof of the station has become a public park with seating, fountains, manicured patches of grass and flowers, and a massive flag of India. It attracts many people', they said. 'Being an interchange station, people travel to Rajiv Chowk via various metro lines, and take a little more time out for their necessary transfer by going above ground to meet each other.' However, a closer look at the use of spaces above and around other metro stations led the students to conclude that Rajiv Chowk is an exceptional case. 'Most stations fail miserably in being more than a logistical hub.'

NO WANDERING

The Metro generally provides the most economical connection between two places in the city – both in terms of time and money. The routes are clear and direct – it is a hard system to get lost in. Although it would seem that these are features the marketing department of the Metro should use to advertise its success, some students noted that this speed and clarity also has at least one negative side effect. 'The system leaves little scope for wandering', they lamented. 'The chances of unexpectedly discovering parts of the city that fall outside of its mega-grid have been reduced quite a bit.'

FORMAL ZONES OF INFORMALITY

In similar vein, another group of students, discussing the reduced place of informal systems in the context of the metro, expressed regret at the disappearance of 'soft edges', spheres of informality and 'unexpectedness'. They contended that if too much structure is imposed on human activity and informality disappears with it, places tend to fail. But can we design infrastructure in such a way that it accommodates the informal? Can there be a system that is sufficiently organized, yet allows interventions? They suggested creating zones of informality around metro stations. 'Different zones would have different functions and would give users different experiences', one student explained. They proposed making the immediate area surrounding the metro station into a vendor zone. The next zone could be the cycle rickshaw and auto rickshaw zone. 'We think that such zones will allow informal systems to thrive, while simultaneously increasing the amount of secure space for women after sunset. These zones will provide a gradual transition from a high-security metro station to vacant, dark surroundings. In such an environment, women, when they get off the trains and hire a rickshaw or auto, will feel and indeed be more secure than in the current set-up.'

ALTERNATIVE FUNCTIONS

For about four hours each night the Metro comes to a halt. Several students looked at the possible alternative functions for the metro system during these hours. The most straightforward alternative function would be to have it transport goods at hours it doesn't transport passengers, they felt. It would not just maximize the use of the existing infrastructure, but would also help to decongest

Delhi's roads at night. 'Anyone who has driven between the massive trucks on the roads of Delhi at night would surely welcome alternative ways for goods to reach their destination', one student explained.

Other, more unexpected, ideas included using the stations to run night schools, having site-specific performances at stations and in trains, and transforming the coaches into moving exhibition spaces.

THE FUTURE

Excited to see students participating with such enthusiasm in the workshop and, moreover, to see their ability to come up with so many diverse and creative ideas in the short span of the exercise, we can only say that we really look forward to seeing their work in the fields of planning and architecture in the future!

SCHOOL OF PLANNING AND ARCHITECTURE, DELHI

ARCHITECTURE AS CRAFT

ROMI KHOSLA

Romi Khosla (1941) is a double graduate of Cambridge University (Economics) and The Architectural Association in London. Upon his return to India in 1972 he established the design firm Romi Khosla Design Studios. His son, Martand Khosla, followed in his footsteps and joined the firm as a partner in 2001.

Khosla's projects are found all over India, as well as several other countries, including Nepal and the Netherlands. They also span all types of projects. Khosla has designed large recreational and educational complexes (including a boarding school built on a 200-acre plot), boutique hotels, a gallery, private houses and corporate headquarters. In 2014, his design for the corporate offices of Volvo-Eicher in India was awarded the LEEDS Platinum Green Rating.

In addition to practising architecture, Khosla worked as a Principal Consultant to UNDP, UNOPS, UNESCO, and WTO. In this capacity he carried out several Urban Planning, Revitalisation and Tourism Planning missions to the Balkans, Cyprus, Central Asia, and Tibet. He was invited to act as jury member for the Aga Khan Awards and nominated a trustee of The India Foundation for the Arts. He has also published a wide variety of articles and several books. In *Buddhist Monasteries in the Western Himalaya* (1978) he shared experiences of his treks on foot into the deepest valleys of the inner Himalayas. Other titles of his include *The Loneliness of the Long Distant Future* (2005) and *The Idea of Delhi* (1998).

Craft, we hear frequently during our visits to the South Delhi office of Romi Khosla. Khosla, his partner (and son) Martand Khosla and some twenty staff's commitment to treat architecture as a craft is the recurring theme in all our conversations. Their commitment is reflected in the type of projects taken on by the office ('We generally avoid commercial work'), and from the extent to which models are used ('Everything we do is modelled and based on these models we develop our ideas'). The commitment also resounds in the architect's views on architecture in India, on what is valuable in Indian architecture and what is not. Khosla feels you can't learn much from Indian architecture as you encounter it in cities today. It is the rural areas we should learn from. 'In the villages you will find interesting solutions in wood, intriguing ways of adapting buildings to the weather, ample display of traditional craftsmanship and sustainable practice.' But most of all the emphasis on craftsmanship shows from how Khosla and his partner avoid using architectural elements produced in factories. 'Nowadays if I design a building I can ring a number and they can deliver the entire façade to me', Khosla explains. 'Similarly I can ring other numbers for all the other components. But this is not architecture.' He prefers to craft his buildings–in design and in execution.

Treating architecture as a craft does not mean the use of technology is banned, though. 'I can still use low and high technology', Khosla says. 'In India I generally opt for low-level technology. But for projects in Europe we chose to use high-level technology. Our Twist & Shout project in Rotterdam is an example of a project where we used high-level technology. We used wood and steel. But still it is crafted.'

PERSONAL FAVOURITES

'Architects are always happy to show you their best work', says Khosla. 'Often it is one of their latest buildings, as when one gets older one tends to make fewer mistakes. You simply know your materials better and that increases the chances of getting it right. Yet one of my favourite buildings is one of the first I did back in the 1970s: a house in Manali. In some ways it resembled traditional ways of building, in its choice of materials, for example. It was made entirely of stone and wood. But in many other ways it is an example of using traditional crafts to do something new.'

Another favourite of his is the Volvo-Eicher Headquarters in Gurgaon. Although at first sight it seems the two designs could not be further apart in typology, Khosla quickly points out to us the consistency in his work over the span of four decades. 'This project, even though mostly done in steel, was as much crafted as the wooden house: the whole steel façade was made by hand and welded in custom-made style.'

HISTORY: DELHI PLANNING

Rather than discussing architecture in New Delhi at length, Khosla thinks our topic of conversation should be planning in Delhi. 'Because Delhi is all about planning', he says.

'The layout of Shahjahanabad, the area we call Old Delhi today, is a perfect example of utopian planning. It is entirely based on the concept of the paradise garden. Chandni Chowk was a central vista with a water course surrounded by gardens, and the entire city was enclosed by walls. The defeat of the Mughal Empire and the start of British Rule heralded in many ways a new era, of urban planning. What [Albert] Speer did for Berlin, [Edwin] Lutyens did for Delhi', Khosla summarizes the immediate effect on the infrastructure and layout of the Indian capital. 'Through gateways, central avenues, and radial connections, the British architect and planner connected all the former incarnations of Delhi.'

Lutyens simultaneously introduced new ideas and practices in residential building. 'Taking inspiration from the ideas of Ebenezer Howard, Lutyens put the main building in the centre of a plot, while keeping the ground around it open. This was a full reversal of the traditional layout used in India: where buildings surround a courtyard.'

'The reasons for these innovations were not only political but also addressed the Colonial obsession about security', Khosla continues. 'In 1857 the British rulers faced the same problem as [Georges-Eugene] Haussmann faced in Paris. The British were unable to fight the rebels as they couldn't access Old Delhi. Open avenues would fix that problem. They said that increased access was required to deliver services, but in reality it was for their armies, and thereby to decrease the chance of rebellion. Lutyens, being part of the Garden City movement, was not randomly selected. His wife was a niece of the ... ex-viceroy. The Viceroy knew he hadn't hired an urban architect, but one specialized and interested in designing garden houses and garden cities.'

Returning to Delhi's present incarnation after visiting Mughal and British Delhi, we ask what the city is like today, according to Khosla. He does not hesitate. 'It is the biggest trickster city', he says, using the phrase from the title of a popular bundle of essays on the Indian capital.[1] 'Nothing and no-one here is straightforward. Everyone plays tricks. Real estate is only one example. It is being sold as a trick. They sell it as Malibu Heights, Wellington Estate, Paradise Island ... !'

THREE LEVELS

To come to terms with this trickster city in which he lives and works, the architect feels he needs to look at it at different levels. He takes ample time to explain his approach in detail and warmly recommends all architects and planners adopt the same. 'We should try to look at the city through three different lenses', he starts. 'We will notice different things and draw different conclusions each time and really get to understand the urban area in which we live and work.'

'Most architects and urban planners confine themselves to looking at the city through one lens: that which observes the obvious level. Does it work? Does it not work? Can we quick-fix it? There is never enough pedestrian space. There are always too many cars. We can talk about those obvious aspects of the city, of any city, without a problem with those who live and work in other contexts.'

'Next comes the deeper level. At this level urban governance becomes an issue. We get embroiled with the perceptions of urban managers on what the city has to be. Looking at the city at this level means that the image of the city will appear to break up. We get involved with counter-images of the city, for instance from slum areas. As an outsider it is valuable to engage with the city at this level. You will start to consider different things. You will see that there is not one object, but many different ones.'

'The last level, the hidden level is the hardest to gauge. It requires becoming aware of aspects that are not easily uncovered and that require real investigation. We find a lot of corruption at this level: developers that influence building laws, black money changing hands ... It is about agendas being controlled by forces that never show their face. No newspaper bluntly says: 'This Minister has been heavily bribed by so and so to change the bye-laws.' Yet, to understand the city and to understand what is happening there, we have to take these aspects into account as well.'

VALIDATION

After a sip of tea, Khosla continues: 'Just looking at these levels is not enough, we should verify our findings as well. Validating our observations and analyses becomes progressively harder for each level. If I am saying there is not enough pedestrian space, I can take fifty photographs to prove my observation is correct. At the deeper level I will have to show there is no area planning, which already takes more effort. At the hidden level, I may point to the caste system and its effect that no one really cares about the poor. 'You want to sell your wares? Find yourself a place, even if on the sidewalk.' To validate my observation of the callous attitude of the middle classes towards the poor, I would have to ask questions, talk with NGOs, with researchers. Have they noticed the same as I did? Just taking photographs won't do.'

CHANGE

The point of looking at the city through this framework is to better understand the city and to be able to create the right kind of change. 'I think architects work in one of the few professions where we think about the need for change, talk about it, and create it', says Khosla. 'As architects we all operate on three levels. We just need to be more conscious about it, so that we can come up with better solutions.'

In addition, Khosla feels that architects and planners–despite seeing plenty of unthoughtful, hurried and unsustainable development around them–should not grow cynical. 'Even if you don't agree with the people on that big boat rushing it all, you really only have two choices: being cynical, or saying there are other ways.' Arguing there are other ways will keep your mind alive, Khosla says. 'It forces you to be creative and continually on the verge of coming up with new ideas. It is important for us to offer an alternative; more important than being cynical.'

[1] **SHVETA SHARDA (2010)** *Trickster City: Writings from the Belly of the Metropolis*. Delhi: Penguin.

VOLVO-EICHER HEADQUARTERS, GURGAON

JMI UNIVERSITY CANTEEN, DELHI

TWIST & SHOUT, ROTTERDAM, THE NETHERLANDS

SKYLINE OF OLD DELHI

MY DELHI
ROMI KHOSLA

DELHI IS SPECIAL BECAUSE

Presently Delhi is the closest approximation to how Indian urbanism ought to be. Cities should be greener, like Delhi is. They should not focus on high-rise; Delhi is essentially a low-rise city. Of course, there are problems, but they are due to scale. If you would have to settle one million people in a Bombay-type settlement or a Delhi-type setting the choice is easy.

THIS CAN BE IMPROVED

Every politician should keep his fingers off the Master Plan. The problem is that they want money, and real estate is a quick way to get it. These politicians change land-use regulations. They allow builders to build higher. They don't respect the Master Plan. They only respect their bank balance. The Master Planner in Delhi is used as doorman: to clean your shoes on before you go in.

MY FAVOURITE PLACE

Lodhi Gardens, because it is different from other parks and because it symbolises India. It's different because it is the symbol of the 'juxtapositioning' of many landscape ideas. It starts as a series of tombs. Then the British make it into Lady Willingdon Park, by putting a wall around it and allowing British couples to come there in the evening to smooch and walk in the evenings. Later, the Indian government gets a Japanese landscape designer to work on the park, and finally the Public Works Department decides to let gardeners plant whatever they feel like! The end result: the ultimate disrespectful landscape garden. India has great capabilities to disrespect things: architecture, democracy, governance, and landscape gardens. So to me, this park really is India.

THE BEST PLACE TO RELAX

On a soft mat on the floor and getting a massage from a person who knows how to do it. He would be trained by wrestling discipline, that is, he understands the body and its capacity.

READY FOR DEMOLITION

Most of the low-cost housing that has been done by the Delhi Development Authority. These boxes disrespect the people who are supposed to occupy them. They disconnect between the way they live and their way of living. They poor can live in very dense spaces. The lanes between the houses can be kept small, because they don't own a car. But the houses need to be on the ground floor. They have a way of living that needs them to use the outside much more. They have large families. They prepare food outside. They have a social life that takes place outside, the husbands chatting to their neighbours. If you put them up in high floors, you isolate them. You break them down. You control them.

FAVOURITE DELHI BOOK

William Dalrymple's *City of Djinns*. I love the idea of someone from outside India coming and commenting on us. Some of the best books have been written by people who came to live here. Indians are good at navel gazing.

IF I HAD TO CHOOSE BETWEEN DELHI OR ANY OTHER CITY I WOULD SELECT

I would live in the mountains, not in a city. Calcutta is decaying. Bombay is overcome with social problems. Madras is too alien for me, too far away. Bangalore is a terrible built environment: you can't walk there.

WHAT WE CAN LEARN FROM DELHI

Delhi showcases the great role that architects can play in a city. There is a great contrast between rubbish built by bad architects and terrific work by good architects, making no distinction between Indian or non-Indian architects, by the way. Non-Indians have done wonderful institutional buildings as well. It is not about being Indian. It is about the quality of architecture. It is about respect. India should respect its architects the way it respect its film stars.

BACK TO BASICS

PANKAJ VIR GUPTA & CHRISTINE MUELLER

Christine Mueller (1973) studied Architecture at Washington University in St Louis and at Harvard University Graduate School of Design.

Pankaj Vir Gupta (1970) studied Architecture at the University of Virginia and Yale University.

The partners founded vir.mueller architects in 2003. The firm combines architectural research, education, and practice. Prior to establishing the firm Mueller worked at Office dA in Boston. As a student Gupta worked for Stein, Doshi, and Bhalla in New Delhi. After graduation he worked at Will Bruder Architects in Arizona, USA.

In 2006 they shifted to India and established a full-time architectural office in New Delhi.

The work of vir.mueller architects has been widely published and awarded–in North America, in Europe, and in India. Awards include those received from the American Institute of Architects, the Foundation for World Education, the George Nakashima Foundation for Peace, and the Graham Foundation for Advanced Studies in the Fine Arts.

Pankaj Vir Gupta and Christine Mueller, founders of vir.mueller architects, state on their website that they 'accord primacy to the process of design'. Their work, however, does not end the day they hand over their drawings. They emphasize that for them 'projects are only deemed complete once they have been constructed'. As a result, the process of building is closely monitored by the architects. This extended quality control has led to them feeling 'super proud of every single thing we have built'. Over cups of green tea, Gupta and Mueller explain to us why this is no mean feat. 'The quality of contractors we have to work with in Delhi is far from guaranteed', Gupta begins. 'Just like in the West, Indian clients will bait their projects with various contractors and often the cheapest bidder is awarded the project. But in India, unlike in the West, not every contractor has a baseline quality', he says. 'Nevertheless, we don't have our own workers, like some boutique architecture firms do, but we take an ordinary team of construction workers and work with them. We are learning to work with even the worst. We work with them so intensively and with such focus that the same brick mason who built that dirty wall over there, that is already falling apart, can now build a beautiful brick screen on our project for us.'

GYMNASTICS

How do they do it? How do they reach the quality they are known for and so deservedly proud of? Gupta compares it to making haute cuisine in a fast-food restaurant kitchen. 'To do that our process has to be very much in synchronicity with our ability to execute. With plenty of patience, and plenty of rigorous research thrown in. We spend a significant amount of time on site making mock-ups and translations of our detailed drawings to real life. We keep our detailing one on one. We take a good look at the person who will construct it. What does he usually do? Then we figure out how we can adjust what he normally does, in order to make him really sing. We look at it as if it's gymnastics. We make him stretch: a little more ... a little more ... Until he is outside his comfort zone, but within a zone in which we can control him. We train him intellectually to understand the consequence of what we are requesting him to build.'

Unfortunately, the training's impact often does not last beyond the project, Mueller admits. 'You would expect that when they work with the next architect, they would have become much better, and they can replicate the quality achieved with us. But no–they don't. The problem is that the baseline of aspiration in India for design and construction is very low. Until we raise that entire conversation to a different level, we will be on this very microscopic one-on-one kind of trajectory.' What motivates them to keep investing so much energy is concern about the example they would set if they don't build well.

CRITICISM AND COMPLIMENTS

In 2006 Gupta and Mueller moved to India from the USA, where they first studied and later practised architecture, and held teaching positions as well. Although they find it important to be in Delhi ('It is about having an impact on people who otherwise have no access to that impact'), and do not plan to return to America, they admit they 'need' their regular visits. Every other semester Gupta teaches at the School of Architecture at the University of Virginia. Interestingly, there, far away from his Delhi home, he is leading a three year research and design investigation on the relationship between New Delhi and its river, the Yamuna.

'The intellectual component of exchanges about architecture in India is limited', he says. 'The conversations are generally very polite and geared towards validation. There is a tendency to deify a person if he or she does something a little better than others. The atmosphere in the USA is much more critical. There I meet fifty architects and we all discuss what we are doing. For everything you show, you get fifteen very hard questions. I need this peer feedback and the interactions during teaching to keep my brain going. They help me to make sense of what we are doing here in a more critical way.'

Gupta and Mueller aspire to change the lack of critical discourse in Delhi by training their staff rigorously. 'Everyone who now works for us should start their own office', says Mueller. 'That is the way to create a parallel track. They can't afford to go to Harvard, but here they get the best critical training. They should be better than us in several years.'

There is one more reason why Gupta and Mueller enjoy teaching in America. 'America makes me feel like a rock star', Gupta says laughing. 'Any time I give a lecture in the USA on our work I feel like I should be hanging out with Bono and Sting.

They make you feel so special for building what you are building. They tell us our work is unique, as it is highly crafted, articulate architecture. We also hear that our work is special, as it is so textured and craftsman-like, yet somehow legible to the contemporary canon.'

LEARNING FROM

The partners enjoy working in Delhi, but are not uncritical of how the city operates. 'Singapore in 1960 was not very different from Delhi in 1960', says Gupta. 'But Singapore had a vision and made conscious decisions about the development of the city: decisions regarding housing, drinking water, infrastructure. Delhi should have a vision. As a capital city it should aspire to be an example of how cities ought to be, like Chandigarh does. You may agree or disagree with the ideas behind Chandigarh, but at least Nehru had an urban vision. Delhi, on the contrary, really shows the rest of the country how not to be, what can go wrong when you have no vision. You can learn from Delhi that ignoring problems is not a solution; that you can't have cities prosper through denial.'

Delhi also has a few lessons to teach about elitism, Gupta feels. 'India's power structure is mapped onto the spatial structure of Delhi to a ridiculous extent. India's most powerful people occupy what is a completely non-sustainable zone: Lutyens' Delhi.' Gupta suggests it might be time to ask some critical questions about this set-up. 'Should those who intend to serve 1.3 billion people have a five-acre garden in the middle of the capital city? Should they even be given housing? Shouldn't they actually have to go out and find their own accommodation?'

WORKERS' HOUSING

Apart from making an impact with the questions they ask out loud, the quality of construction, and the critical training of their staff, vir.mueller aspires to make a mark with the type of projects they take on. They wish to create 'enough of an echo to change aspirations'. Their housing for agricultural farm workers in rural Punjab is a good example.

'It's part of a larger master plan of about a hundred acres', Gupta shares, while instructing a colleague to fetch the project drawings. 'Our master plan covers the landowner's house, housing for the farm workers, their bathhouse, a cattle shed, and a storage area. Before making decisions on which building would be constructed where, we assessed how the space is and will be used. We studied a wide variety of questions: How can workers discretely take a bath in the bathhouse? How can their security be ensured? How do they go from feeding the cattle to the orchard where oranges are sorted? We looked at the direction of the wind and the entrances to make sure the buildings are not just well-ventilated, but also optimally located in relation to where manure should be stored. We acknowledged that the workers have children who need to play, so we allowed for a dedicated play area, rather than having them to play in spaces frequently used for other purposes, such as drying clothes. Before deciding on the location of the animal sheds we studied where the cattle will be milked, and how the cows will return to their shelter.

'I think few other architect would spend this kind of intellectual capital on reconceptualizing human and animal habitation on remote farms somewhere in rural India', Gupta continues. 'The normal approach is to simply construct a shed for the farm workers. This landlord may have been the first to hire an architect to design their houses. Ultimately, it can show other landowners that the people who work for them, on their hundreds of acres of farmland, can be housed in a better way. Even if it is still just in small four-metre wide buildings on one acre of land, it is not a tent, a dirty shack, or alongside a wall. Thus, our work is questioning the attitude that architects can't design for the lowest economic levels of society.'

RETURN TO THE BASICS

Although the architects probably spent more time on research than average, the emphasis within the firm remains on practising architecture. Says Mueller: 'At the end of the day we need a real site and a real client. We want a real local context. Only then does it become worthwhile for us to spend time on it. We could have made a much more dramatic roof for our workers' houses, but the cheapest way to make a prefabricated structure with a column base is that way. The way we did it, with that span.'

Working on a real project, in a real location, meant having to select real materials to work with as well. The remote location of the farm with the workers' houses influenced the choice of materials as well as some of the design choices. 'We built the entire building out of local brick. The windows come in just two sizes, since a carpenter makes them with his bare hands, working on site. We did not use glass in any of the constructions, as it is not locally available. Replacing a broken glass pane would mean a new one having to be cut and conveyed to the site from a town 150 kilometres away, over a bumpy road. The windows have a screen and a wooden shutter instead.'

The project had unexpected consequences for the architects. They started to question material and design choices in other assignments as well. 'We started to ask ourselves: "If we can do it that simple here in rural Punjab ... then why do we need to use six materials in Delhi?" With architecture becoming more and more whimsical, we are beginning to say it may be time to return to the basics. Working in rural contexts and with small budgets influences how we design for Delhi and other places.'

FARM WORKERS HOUSING PROJECT IN ABOHAR, PUNJAB

INSTITUTE OF ENGINEERING AND TECHNOLOGY AT AHMEDABAD UNIVERSITY

DEFENCE COLONY RESIDENCE, DELHI

SAXANA APARTMENTS, DELHI

INDIA GATE GARDENS FOUNTAIN, DELHI

MY DELHI
VIR GUPTA & MUELLER

DELHI IS SPECIAL BECAUSE

Delhi is not a boutique city. It's a city with many textures and many scales of economy. It is a super-city. There are only a few cities in the world with such intensity. Taking Delhi as a canvas to practise [architecture] we could exhaust our lifetimes easily.

THIS CAN BE IMPROVED

People's sense of civic pride can be greatly improved, as well as the relationships between the citizens of Delhi. There are signs of change, though. We saw an outrage when someone got raped on a bus in in the city. It was not the first time that someone was raped in Delhi, but suddenly it just crossed that line. More and more people want to be and start to feel empowered, they want more control, and have started to raise their voices regarding the issues in the city. Those who are in charge have to respond. This is an important development. It means citizens are starting to act more like citizens.

READY FOR DEMOLITION

This is a very loaded question. To make sound decisions you would need absolutely clear and simple and objective rules that do not allow any discrimination based on economic or other factors. For example, anything that doesn't survive an earthquake of 5.5 on Richter's scale should be demolished. If that means monuments and heritage buildings will fall, well maybe it's their time? But having survived for centuries, the monuments would easily outlive some of the more recently built buildings of poor quality. Maybe it's enough to let two of those buildings remain and maybe it is not sustainable to have so many as we have now? The key is to point to basic things that no one can argue with: risk of fire, of earthquake, the need for water, for sanitation ...

MY FAVOURITE DELHI BOOK

One of my favourites is *Old Delhi-New York: Personal Views*, by C.S.H. Jhabvala. He was an architect who used to teach drawing at the SPA here in Delhi in the 60s and 70s, and later became the Head of Architecture at the same institute. Jhabvala put New York and Delhi on the same plane and spoke most evocatively about the cities through his drawings. He made his arguments from an experiential point of view: he lived half his life in New Delhi and the last 35 years in New York.

MY FAVOURITE RESTAURANT

There are so many great restaurants in this city. But if I have to name just three I would say Potbelly, the Bihari restaurant in Shahpur Jat, the Lodhi Garden restaurant where you dine under the trees and Tres. The chef at the latter is very good.

MY FAVOURITE PLACE

Humayun's Tomb and Lodhi Gardens. It is so familiar to me: I grew up in that neighbourhood.

MY FAVOURITE DELHI FILM

There is a Hindi movie from the 1980s that was filmed in Delhi: *Chashme Buddoor*. I saw it again recently, and noticed that it is beautifully filmed and shows a lot of Delhi as a garden city. It is about some young people who live together in a tiny room. Because they are housed in such cramped quarters a lot of their life takes place in the city's spaces: in gardens, parks, and on the streets. The film shows how in the 1970s Delhi really was a garden city with ample room for life to take place in the public realm-the mark of urban success.

MY FAVOURITE BUILDING

I think I probably have the same favourite building as most other architects you spoke to: the India Internatonal Center. That and the Triveni Kala Sangam. Both are really beautiful. Joseph Stein understood how to build in contemporary India better than anyone else practising in his generation.

ACKNOWLEDGEMENTS

This is the second volume in the series Learning from India. The first volume, *Learning from Mumbai*, was completed in 2013. The first copy was presented to the Indian Minister of Urban Development Kamal Nath by Dutch Minister of Infrastructure and the Environment Melanie Schultz van Haegen in Scheveningen on the occasion of the signing of a new Memorandum of Understanding (MoU) on technical cooperation in the field of Spatial Planning, Water Management, and Mobility Management. The positive reactions, support, and intellectually stimulating interactions we had with so many people in the Netherlands and India while producing this first volume made us eager to continue the project and shift our focus to Delhi.

Between April 2013 and November 2014 we visited Delhi three times and were rewarded with a multitude of interesting meetings with urban planners, architects, and other professionals working in some way or the other on or with the city.

We asked photographer Bas Losekoot to join us during one of our visits. We are very grateful that he accepted the invitation and proud to present his wonderful photographs of Delhi in a dedicated photo essay, as well as throughout the book as illustrations.

During the last visit we conducted a design workshop on the spatial impact of the Metro in Delhi. for students of the School of Planning and Architecture (SPA) in Delhi. We would like to warmly thank the participating students for sharing their ideas, the Head of the Department of Architecture of the SPA, Professor Mandeep Singh PhD, for welcoming us to his institute, and arch-i for their organizational help.

We are very grateful to the architects, urban planners, and other professionals who took the time to meet us and allowed us to interview them: Ambrish Arora, Joeri Aulman, Ashok Bhalotra, Anne Feenstra, Mohit Gujral, Romi Khosla, Pradip Krishen, Barjor Mehta, Christine Mueller, Madhav Raman, Sonali Rastogi, Raj Rewal, Onno Ruhl, Mohammad Shaheer and Pankaj Vir Gupta.

Ashok Bhalotra, Shyam Khandekar and Dunu Roy made this volume all the more valuable with their reflective articles that open the book. We are very grateful for these contributions.

We further would like to warmly thank for their help and support the following individuals: Jagriti Arora, Jaydeep Gareja, Kushal Lachhwani, Himanshu Lal, Tanvi Maheshwari, Ridhima Mehrotra, Rohan Patankar, Pritha Samantha, Saumitra Sinha (ArchI), Nazanin Hedayati and Martijn Oskam (Creative Industries Fund NL), Bipin Shah (Mapin Publishing), Sunay Gandhi, Olivia Gandhi, Georgina Grant, Eloise Sky Scholte, Caroline Waltman and Gloria Waltman.

Last, but certainly not least, we want to warmly thank David Raats (DJ Translations, Subtitling & Editing), and our graphic designer Ilse van Klei.

Pelle Poiesz
Gert Jan Scholte
Sanne Vanderkaaij Gandhi

NATIONAL COOPERATIVE DEVELOPMENT CORPORATION (NCDC), DELHI

NEHRU PLACE, DELHI

BAJAJ CAPITAL
BAJAJ CAPITAL
BAJAJ CAPITAL
DELL

LED
टी.टी.
गारमेन्ट्स